MW00995569

THE ROOT BEER BOOK

A Celebration of America's Best-Loved Soft Drink

By Laura E. Quarantiello

LIMELIGHT BOOKS

Copyright (c) 1997 by Tiare Publications

All rights reserved. No part of this book may be reproduced or trans-
mitted in any form or by any means electronic or mechanical, including photocopying, recording or by information storage or retrieval
systems, without permission in writing from the publisher, except by
a reviewer who may quote brief passages in a review.

Book design by John C. Herkimer
Next Wave Graphics, Caledonia, NY

Published by LimeLight Books,
a division of Tiare Publications
P.O. Box 493, Lake Geneva WI 53147.

ISBN: 0-936653-78-7
Printed in the United States of America.

Neither the author nor the publisher assume any liability
whatsoever with respect to the use of the information
presented within this book.

Library of Congress Cataloging-in-Publication Data

Quarantiello, Laura E., 1968-
    The root beer book : a celebration of America's best-loved soft
  drink / by Laura E. Quarantiello.
        p.   cm.
    Includes bibliographical references (p.).
    ISBN 0-936653-78-7 (pbk.)
    1. Carbonated beverages.   I. Title.
  TP630.Q37   1997
  663'.62--dc21   97-3954
                                                                CIP

 CONTENTS

Acknowledgments 5
Introduction 7
Off the Shelf: Modern Root Beers 9
At the Root of it All: The Birth of Root Beer 15
From Sassafras to Synthetics: Root Beer Ingredients 23
Taste Tests: Which Root Beer is Best? 37
Basement Brewing: Making Your Own Root Beer 43
Drips and Drops: Root Beer as a Hobby 51
Root Beer Adventures 55
Root Beer Recipes 59
Important Events in the Development of Soft Drinks 75
Facts About Soft Drinks 77
Soft Drink Brand Introductions in the U.S. 79
Some Root Beer Brands 81
Root Beer on the Internet 85
Root Beer Collector's Magazines and Organizations 87
Beverage Supply Outlets 89
Books of Interest 91

 # ACKNOWLEDGMENTS

No one writes in a vacuum. There is always a silent and too seldom acknowledged or appreciated contingent behind the person who actually puts the words on the paper. This is my chance to say thank you to my own personal silent contingent.

Gerry Dexter, publisher and friend, whose enthusiasm, hard work and research assistance was and is unequaled; Reed D. Andrew of the Society of Root Beer Cans and Bottles; David and Kathy Nader, publishers of the Root Beer Float, for a helping hand in understanding root beer collectibles; Cadbury Beverages Communications and Public Affairs, for outstanding research assistance; Nancy Thiele, Communications Coordinator, 7UP RC Bottling Company of Southern California, Inc.; Pepsi-Cola Company; Coca-Cola Company; Food and Drug Administration, Center for Food Safety and Applied Nutrition; and the National Soft Drink Association.

Any mistakes or inaccuracies in this book are my fault, not theirs.

A Celebration of America's Best-Loved Soft Drink

 **INTRODUCTION**

"There is more similarity in a precious painting by Degas and a frosted mug of root beer than you ever thought possible."

– A. Alfred Taubman
Owner of 550 A&W Root Beer Stands

Americans have are crazy about soft drinks. These fizzy, tasty beverages have crossed all cultural, financial and linguistic lines to become universal refreshments and thirst quenchers extraordinaire. Ninety-five percent of Americans regularly drink them, and today you will find cans and bottles in the hands of rich and poor, young and old. In fact, the popularity of soft drinks in this country makes the United States the world leader in the soft drink industry. Not only do we manufacture more soft drinks than any other country in the world, we also sell more. In 1995 alone soft drink retail sales reached $52 billion, according to the National Soft Drink Association (NSDA). PepsiCo, Inc., estimates that the average person consumes more than fifty-one gallons of soft drinks each year. That's not cans or glasses, folks, that's gallons! They should know; PepsiCo's beverage growth rate increased seven percent in 1995, while rising eleven percent internationally. Their beverage division had net sales just two percent less than their restaurant division (which counts Taco Bell, Kentucky Fried Chicken, and Pizza Hut among its major holdings). Coca-Cola reported that carbonated beverages generated more than three-quarters of their volume performance in 1995.

The carbonated soft drink business continues to grow as companies diversify and new beverages arrive to tease and tantalize the taste buds of consumers. NSDA reports that the soft drink market in the United States currently includes nearly 450 different soft drinks! Competition among soft drink makers is ongoing and fierce, as one look at the appropriate aisle in any supermarket will testify. Greeting the eye are row upon row of colorfully designed cans, bottles and cases, all fighting for your attention. Coca-Cola, Pepsi, Mountain Dew, Slice, Dr. Pepper, dark sodas, clear sodas, cherry sodas - the choice has left many a consumer wandering up and down the aisle, trying to decide which one to buy. One type of soda, however, defies the confusion, and escapes the cola craze. It's an old stand-by, one that even your great-great-grandmother would recognize in a heartbeat - root beer!

While researching this book I asked everyone I met, from my doctor to my priest to the guy I buy my gasoline from, what they knew about root beer. Every single one of them said that while they didn't know a whole lot about it, they did know one thing for sure: they liked to drink it. Some remembered their parents brewing root beer in tall bottles in the basement, some remembered drinking it with vanilla ice cream on hot summer days, but all of them knew what it was. Say what you will about the popularity of Coke and Pepsi, quote me statistics if you must, but I believe that root beer may well be America's best-loved soft drink. You will find it bottled under various brand names - A&W, Dad's, Hires, Barq's, Mug, IBC, Stewart's and a over hundred others - in cans, glass bottles and plastic bottles, on the shelves in every food store, beverage shop or "quick stop" place you visit. Root beer endures as the little soda that could, quietly selling and being enjoyed without fanfare and without large advertising campaigns. When sip comes to gulp, you will find root beer in the glass.

This book is intended as a celebration of root beer, from its beginnings as a medicinal tea introduced to the New World by the Spaniards, to the first brews and beyond, all the way to today's root beers. You'll also discover how easy it is to brew up a batch of your own. I hope you'll enjoy this book as you would a frosty, ice cold mug of root beer: slowly, with your feet up.

A Celebration of America's Best-Loved Soft Drink

OFF THE SHELF: MODERN ROOT BEERS

odern root beer is truly an amazing thing. The next time you're in the beverage section of a grocery store, stop and ponder the long and varied lineage of this drink...and just look where root beer is now. From its humble and somewhat obscure beginnings it has grown and grown and grown still more. Today it is a full-fledged member of the multi-billion dollar soft drink industry.

A 1993 survey conducted by *Beverage Industry* magazine showed that sales of the seven biggest root beer brands had grown to 219.2 million cases, up from 141.7 million in 1986.The numbers show that root beer is holding its own and even moving forward in an industry where the competition is more than fierce. *Supermarket News* magazine reported in early 1996 that soft drink producers were going back to the roots (as it were), marketing their root beer brands heavily during that year. Cadbury Schweppes Beverages is reported to have spent over ten million dollars in 1995 on advertising for their A&W brand alone. That number was expected to increase in 1996, a tactical move expected because of the acquisition of Barq's Root Beer by the Coca-Cola Company. Barqs, and PepsiCo's Mug, both weigh in at just under five million dollars spent for 1995 advertising. Look for all of these statistics to rise as root beer popularity explodes.

Megan Pryor, who serves as vice president of new business at Pepsi-Cola Company, told *Beverage Industry* that beverage marketing wars have always been fierce, but the biggest battle today is within the so-called "quiet beverage" categories, such as root beer. Quiet beverages are those that traditionally do not receive much advertising, that stay in the background, selling steadily, but never approaching the realm of the big sellers. Root beer marketing will see a lot of action, according to Pryor.

"There seems to be a root beer revolution going on," according to Sam Simpson, president of Cable Car Beverages of Denver, distributors of Stewart's Root Beer. Nearly every major beverage company markets a root beer brand: Coca-Cola has Barq's, Pepsi-Cola has Mug, Cadbury Schweppes has A&W and Hires. Even beer maker Henry Weinhard has jumped into the game with an old-fashioned recipe of their own. "There is a rising tide for certain flavors and drinks," Tom Pirko of the industry consulting firm Bevmark told the *Puget Sound Business Journal.* "Anything with a big flavor, such as root beer and cream soda, will do very well."

Packaged in cans, plastic bottles, glass bottles, six-packs, 12-packs or 24-can cases, root beer has carved its niche and assumed its place in the world of soft drinks. Not only is root beer popular as a refreshing break on a hot day or as an anytime thirst quencher, but also as a non-alcoholic alternative to liquor. College students are ordering it in place of beer, and coffee houses are broadening their menus to include it. Stewart's Root Beer is even being sold to customers at the Hard Rock Cafe. As we move toward the close of the 20th Century, root beer is coming back to popularity; an old favorite made new.

Just how big is root beer? Unfortunately, not as big as its fans would like it to be. Leading soft drinks like Coca-Cola, Pepsi and Dr. Pepper have a firm hold on the top spots in soft drink sales. Root beer is a second cousin to these brands and undoubtedly always will be. Industry watchers and market analysts report - depending on who you talk to - that root beer commands anywhere between 2.4 and 4.3% of the $50 billion U.S. soft drink market; a small percentage, but one that seems to be growing.

The root beer market itself is led by several major brands, many with long histories stretching back to the early days of the drink. At last calculation, Cadbury-Schweppes, Inc. held 30.2% of the root beer market. Barq's came in at number two among major manufacturers with a 24.3% share, followed by Dad's at 23.1%, Mug at 13.4%, Hires at 8.4% with IBC and Ramblin' bringing up the rear. In 1993, A&W, Barq's, Dad's, Mug and Hires combined sold 282.2 million gallons of the drink. The root beer segment of the industry leaped ahead 4.3% in 1993, according to *Beverage Digest,* beating the entire soft drink industry, which was up just 3%.

But, selling root beer - like marketing any other soft drink - isn't always easy. "To get a New Yorker to grab a bottle of root beer, you have to do something special," said Jack Shea, general manager of Crystal Geyser East, a supplier of Virgil's root beer. Shea is not alone in understanding that fact.

Take Barq's, for instance. In 1992, the Barq's brand, long known for its irreverent attitude, began a promotion called the "Soviet Union Going Out of Business Sale." In 1993, they promoted temporary tattoos which they called "Barqtoos," and in 1994 they brought out a "Match the DNA" game played on the O.J. Simpson trial hysteria. Barq's 1995 promotion was known as "Stink-n-Stare," a series of scratch and sniff 3-D puzzles designed to appeal to youth, a segment of society to which root beer is beginning to have more and more appeal. Pepsi-Cola has grown wise to this as well, launching a promotion of its own in the summer of 1996 called "Mug Bugs." One hundred forty restored VW Beetles toured the country in Mug root beer sampling promotions.

As the major soda manufacturers push their existing root beer brands, acquire others, brew up new brands and devise fresh ways of marketing, specialized micro breweries are stepping in to give them a run for their money and challenge them for their customers.

Micro breweries, also known as independents - small manufacturers, often with limited or mail-order only distribution - hand craft their own root beer, creating distinctive flavors that many say rival and sometimes even taste better than those produced by the major brands. These manufacturers have the advantage over the majors because they are not attempting to distribute nationwide. Their clientele is small and they brew only as much as they need to fulfill incoming orders. The advantage here is the amount of time and attention which can be given to the brewing process, something which often escapes the major manufacturers, whose large production needs require a highly automated and faster process. Not only that, but micro breweries are known to use more of the natural root beer ingredients, such as sassafras, burdock, vanilla and honey - ingredients which are sometimes impractical for use in large scale production. Virgil's Root Beer, imported by the Crowley Beverage Corporation in Boston, has this to say about their product: "In the North of England, we brew the best root beer you will ever taste. We begin with crystalline water from the lake district and then brew it with natural ingredients- sassafras, anise, licorice, and pure cane sugar. Each bottle is hand-prepared and then shipped to you from our micro brewery in England." Though micro-brewed root beers hold a very small portion of the entire soft drink market, these brewers are dedicated to using traditional methods and recipes, and the results definitely show.

Between the major and the independents brands, your selection of a root beer isn't going to be an easy one. Later on, we'll talk about what to look for in a root beer. For now, take a look at the following list of root beer brands provided courtesy of Reed D. Andrew and the Society of Root Beer Cans & Bottles. The list is an ever-changing thing, constantly being updated as new brands debut. It was as complete as possible at the time this book went to press. Your additions to the list are always welcome. Please contact the Society at the above address, visit their World Wide Web site at http://www.byu.edu/~rdandrew/ or e-mail them at rdandrew@cougarnet.byu.edu.

A&W
Abita
Adirondack
Albertson's A+
American Classics
American Fare
Americana
Arizona Root Beer Float
Ayer's Sarsaparilla
Barq's
Baumeister
Becker's
Berghoff's
Best Health
Best Yet
Big K
Bi Lo
Black Bear
Blue Sky
Briar's Six Gun
Brick Oven
Buyer's Choice
Can-a-pop
Canfield's
C & C
Chek
Cherryland's Best
Chug's Choice
Classic Selection
Colfax

Cool
Cosmos Cott
Cotton Club
Country Delight
Country Springs
Cragmont
Crystal Dad's
Diamond Head
Dog 'n' Suds
Dominick's
Dominion
Dr. Brown's
Dr. McGillicutty's
Dr. Swett's
Family Dollar
Fastco
Faygo Filbert's
Food Club
Food Lion
Fountain Fresh
Fred's Choice
Frolic
Frostop
Frostie
Giant
Glencourt
Grand Classics
Grandpa Graff's
Green Bay Beverages
Grey's

Hank's
Hansen's Clear
Hansen's Creamy
Health Valley
Henry's
Henry Weinhard's
Hill Country Fare
Hires
Hoffman
Holiday
Howie's
Hytop
Hy Vee
I.B.C.
I.G.A.
Iron Horse
It'sa
Janet Lee
J.C. Grey
Jewel
Jim
Jolly Good
JP Falls Old Philadelphia
Kansas City Sarsaparilla
Keiko
Killebrew
Kings Arms Tavern
Kwik Trip
Lady Lee
Lariat
Laura Lynn
Lost Trail
Lotsa
Lyon's
Mad River
Marquee
Martha's Exchange
Mason's
Master Choice
Meijer
Millstream

Mug
Natural Brew
Naturale 90
Nature's Flavors
Nehi
New Wave
New York Seltzer
North Pride
Old Fashioned
Old Keg
Old Time
Old Towne
Our Compliments
Our Family
Parade
Peninsula
Pirate's Keg
Polar
Pop City
Preferred Selection
President's Choice
Primo
Publix
R.J. Corr
Ramblin'
Randall's
Red Leaf
Red Rock
Regent
Richardson's
Richfood
Ritz
R. J. Corr
Rocky Mountain
Rocky Top
Roundy's
Route 66
Royal Islands
Safeway "Select"
Sam's Choice
Sarsaparilla Root Beer

Schweppes
Sea Way
Shasta
Shopper's
Shopper's Value
Shur Fine
Silver Eagle
Simply Soda
Sioux City Sarsaparilla
Sioux City Birch Beer
Smith's
Snapple
Soho
Spanish Peaks Chug's Choice
Spartan
Sprecher
Spree
Spring Grove
Springtime
Stars
Stars and Stripes
Stewart's
Sugar Creek
Sunny Select
Super Sod

Sure Save
Sweet Valley
Thomas Kemper
Thorofare
Top Pop
Tops
Triple "AAA"
TV
Urge "Rowdy"
Varsity
Vess
Vintage
Virgil's
Watson's
Wegman's
Weis Choice
Western Family
White Cross
Wild West Sarsaparilla
Wildwood
Wind River
Winterbrook
World Classics
76

A Celebration of America's Best-Loved Soft Drink

AT THE ROOT OF IT ALL

The origins of root beer are difficult to trace, for myth and legend seem to have hopelessly intertwined and obscured the trail, at least on the surface. If we probe deeper, however, we find that the origin of root beer is closely tied to the history of medicinal herbs and the very beginnings of pharmacopoeia. We are led straight back through thousands of years of recorded history and beyond, to a time when early man sought to heal the physical illnesses of his life with the only tools he had available. It is here that bits and pieces of the story can be found and, connecting them together, we discover the proud and worthy history of a drink which today we consider " just another" carbonated beverage.

Cave drawings and inscriptions on tablets have long been used by archeologists to give us a glimpse into the world of early man. From these examples of primitive art we have learned how he hunted, defended himself, and survived in a world where the odds were definitely stacked against him. These pictures also tell us that early man suffered illness, injury and disease, such as he would through the succeeding ages and into the present. There were no physicians or surgeons to fix, mend or heal, and there were no pharmacists available to dispense medications. Instead, primitive man was forced to become doctor and druggist to himself, and often his medicinal tools were the wild roots, nuts, berries, leaves, branches and bushes that covered the landscape. It was the beginning of the use of plants as medicines, a practice that would cover thousands if not millions of years, and touch all areas of the world. From stone tablets to papyrus scrolls, the list of healing herbs and plants were recorded and passed along, and information about each area's pharmacopoeia eventually spread across oceans and continents as travel and exploration began. One of the best examples of this is Christopher Columbus, who returned to Barcelona in 1492 and regaled Queen Isabella with stories of the many strange things he had found in the New World, including mysterious plants.

By the late fifteenth and early sixteenth century exploration was in full swing and this led to the swift expansion of commerce. New trade routes opened and imports and exports of such things as timber, furs, skins, tar, jewelry, textiles, oil, wine, fruit and other foods became customary. In Europe it was especially common for explorers, after months and often years away at sea, to sail back into port carrying samples of herbs, spices and plants given to them by the native populations of the places they had explored. Drug plants had long been a popular trade item among older civilizations. The sailors explained that they had seen these herbs and spices made into poultices, ointments, elixirs, pills, teas and other concoctions which were used with great success in the treatment of all manner of illness and disease. Some claimed that they had even been cured by these natural remedies. So began an influx of so-called "miracle plants," a rush of importation and trade that caused a great fascination with botany and natural medicine among Europeans.

Western medicine at the time was very rigid in its belief that illness was the result of an imbalance within one of the three human pillars: mental, emotional or physical. There was a great gulf between the practice of the professional physician and that of the native healer. The physician believed in manipulating the bodily processes through bloodletting, evacuation and purging, while native healers believed in allowing the medicines contained within plants to gently return the body to full health.

However, where Western medicine was failing, native medicine appeared to be succeeding. Spanish sailors in the Caribbean, for instance, were contracting syphilis, which they brought back to Europe. While European physicians struggled to find a cure, West Indian healers used twigs from the guaiac tree, which proved highly successful. In 1508, the first supplies of guaiac were imported from the Caribbean.

Nicholas Monardes, a Seville physician, began to haunt the docks, talking to ship captains about their cargoes. Monardes was highly interested in native medicines derived from plants. He was both intrigued and excited by the new cures and began compiling them into a book and experimenting on his patients with samples of the new drugs. He soon discovered that many were very effective against disease and illness.

Meanwhile, settlers in North America had few doctors to care for them and soon were turning to the Indians for assistance in curing their ills. Native Americans were experts in the use of plants as medicines. They believed that each plant, bush and tree had a special use, a way in which it could help the human body to heal. Not every cure worked, of course, but each one that did was remembered and passed on to others. In the early part of the seventeenth century, John Josselyn, an American from Boston, prepared a book of native remedies in which he told of beers flavored with liquorice, fennel and sassafras. In South America, Spanish colonists were refining their nature treatments, as well as learning new herbal treatments from the Indians there. These plants and their related cures spread, and explorers visiting North and South America brought them back to Europe.

The sheer number of these native drugs and their reputed uses was impressive. For instance, Foxglove (digitalis purpurea) was used against a number of maladies, including tuberculosis. Moneywort (Lysimachia nummularia) was used to stop internal bleeding and to cure whooping cough. St. John's Wort (Hypericum perforatum) found favor as an ointment and as a respiratory ailment cure. Sassafras (Sassafras albidum) was used for all manner of ills, especially intestinal gas and as a diuretic. Wild Indigo (Baptisia tinctoria) root was steeped to make an antiseptic liquid for use on lacerations and abrasions, while Blood Root (Sanguinaria canadensis) found wide use as a relief from dysentery. Many of these cures were prepared by carefully harvesting the roots or leaves of the plant and gently boiling them to extract the essential oils. The resulting tea made a soothing and potentially curative drink.

By the 1800's, a booming business in remedies and cure-alls had sprung up in America, a nation that was pushing further west with every passing day. Drug peddlers worked the backwoods, selling herbal remedies, herbs, spices, roots and bark. Running on the strength of the overwhelming interest in native medicine and the success of the drug peddlers, traveling salesmen began hawking patent medicines, and the traveling medicine show became a popular and frequent attraction in many cities and towns. Some of the shows featured Indians, doctors or professors who would brew up and demonstrate herbal treatments to onlookers, thereby lending a legitimacy to the medicines. Unfortunately, many of these medicines were often nothing more than colored water and sugar, or more commonly, alcohol. Hood's Sarsaparilla was 18% alcohol, while Hostetter's Bitters was 44%. Morphine and opium were other common ingredients. At the height of the patent medicine craze, a peddler could make a million dollars a year hawking these novelty cures.

Many of the popular patent medicines were in liquid form. A sip here, a gulp there, a glass of this or that and you were cured...or at least on your way to better health. In fact, mineral water had long been considered as beneficial to health. More than two thousand years ago, Hippocrates, the "father of medicine," suspected that the Romans and Greeks, who bathed in natural mineral springs bubbling from the earth, were onto something good. It would take another thousand or so years before drinking this naturally carbonated water became popular. In the United States, it was mineral springs in New York state that attracted physicians and chemists who began to study those tiny popping bubbles. Eventually, normal tap water was carbonated through a procedure invented by Englishman Joseph Priestly. Priestly, a chemist, had the good fortune to live next to a brewery, where each day carbon dioxide gases were given off by the beer brewing process. In 1768, Priestly added these byproduct CO_2 gases, which he called fixed air, to mineral water, thereby giving it fizz. Before you could say "it tickles my nose," "soda water" became the tonic of choice. Sold at soda fountains in drug stores across America, soda water latched on to the legacy of the patent medicine and soon became wildly popular.

The increasing competition for customers soon forced store owners to devise new ways of drawing in their clientele, which they did by adding flavoring to straight soda water. Cherry, lemon, peach, strawberry, orange, ginger, grape, pineapple and banana were some of the many different flavors produced. The drinks had many virtues, according to advertisements of the day. They purified and enriched the blood, renewed energy, restored vitality, strengthened the nerves, and aided digestion. Whatever your problem, soda water was the answer. It was a tonic, an elixir, and a new lease on life, all in one eight or 12 ounce glass.

But the competition kept growing, and much like the patent medicine hawkers of the age, soda fountain owners discovered that they were successful only as long as they provided new and varied choices for their demanding customers. The fruit drinks were fine, but they offered limited choices. Something altogether different was needed, something that would excite the public, that would sell better than fruit-flavored soda water. So was born a variety of unique blends

A Celebration of America's Best-Loved Soft Drink

brewed from exotic and sometimes secret ingredients, touted as mysterious old-world concoctions similar to those used by Indians and the natives of foreign lands.

Sadly, history seems to fail us at this point. We know that a wealth of unusual and mysterious new drinks exploded upon the market, but the first of these - if there truly was a first - has not been definitively recorded. We know that Dr. Augustin Thompson created Moxie Nerve Food in 1885, Charles Alderton brewed up Dr. Pepper the same year, and John Pemberton's Coca-Cola debuted in 1886. But, when it comes to root beer, the lineage is even hazier.

David Nader, root beer memorabilia collector and publisher of the *Root Beer Float* newsletter, says that "Charles Hires is generally considered the one who first promoted root beer on a national basis, through the use of trade cards, newspaper advertising, and other means of innovative advertising. As far as being the first to commercially produce root beer, that is a tough one. I don't think that anyone can honestly answer that question. We do know of documentation that exists that a New York brewer by the name of John Dearborn was producing root beer on a commercial basis as early as 1842. His business address was 131 Clinton Street, New York City, according to Alan Schmeiser's out of print book titled *Have Bottles Will Pop*. That date puts John Dearborn about 34 years ahead of Charles Hires. There are many examples of root beer stoneware, or pottery bottles that have a bottler's name, and the words "root beer" on them, that have been documented to be in business in the 1840's, '50's, and '60's, that all predate Hires. The problem with most of these bottlers, or brewers, is that their product was produced and sold on a somewhat local, or regional basis."

The most accurate statement that those of us who study the history of soft drinks can say is that the first widespread commercial soft drink that relied on roots and herbs instead of fruit flavoring may well have been created in 1876 by a Philadelphia Quaker and pharmacist named Charles E. Hires.

Sold to consumers as a solid concentrate designed for home brewing, Hires Herb Tea claimed to contain a combination of sixteen wild roots and berries, including sassafras, spikenard, juniper, wintergreen, pipsissewa, dog grass, sarsaparilla, vanilla, ginger, hops, licorice and birch bark. Hires had acquired the recipe from a country innkeeper's wife in rural New Jersey, where he was honeymooning. After he returned home, the 24-year-old pharmacist employed two professors from a medical college to assist him in developing a formula for turning the drink into a solid concentrate. Adding water, sugar and yeast to the extract produced a beverage very much like the one Hires had tasted at the inn. One packet sold for twenty-five cents and yielded five gallons of the drink.

According to popular legend, Hires was soon advised by the Reverend Russell Conwell, founder of Temple University, that the conservative name Herb Tea would not appeal to the hard-drinking miners of his Philadelphia hometown. No self-respecting liquor drinker was ever going to be caught holding a glass of something called herb tea! If Hires really wanted to create a selling drink, he would have to think of something better. "No, the miners would never drink it if it were called a tea," Conwell told him. "Let's call it a beer - root beer." At the 1876 United States Centennial Exposition, Charles Hires introduced something that he called the "temperance drink...the greatest health giving beverage in the world." Hires Root Beer, is thus a direct descendant of the healing sassafras tea of ages past.

Though Charles Hires may have been the first off the blocks commercially with a root beer drink, he certainly wasn't to be the last. The refreshment quickly became popular, primarily for its taste, but also because the idea of temperance had been steadily growing for quite some time. The push to prohibit the manufacture and sale of alcoholic beverages was becoming a shove as several states began instituting local prohibition regulations. The temperance movement had gone national, and everything was steadily heading toward "going dry." Root beer, with its foamy head and dark gold appearance, looked like real beer, which was so fashionable at the time. So root beer was the natural alternative.

Hires began to advertise his drink aggressively, becoming the first person in history to take out a full page newspaper advertisement. "Doing business without advertising is like winking at a girl in the dark. You know what you are doing, but nobody else does," Hires was quoted as saying. He could clearly see the competition coming and he wasted no time securing his place at the top. One of the first Hires newspaper ads read: "Hires Improved Root Beer. Package 25c. Makes five gallons of a delicious, sparkling, and wholesome beverage. Sold by all druggists or sent by mail on receipt of 25c. C. E. Hires, 48 N. Del. Ave., Philadelphia, PA." Later, the full page ad featured a beautiful blonde holding a glass and sitting on a box with the Hires logo and the caption: "Your Guarantee of Real Root Juices." The text read:

"Delicious, Healthful, Economical. Three Ways to Get Hires Root Beer. At Fountains: When you insist on Hires R.J. Root Beer, you get real root juices, not just oil flavored imitations - yet you pay no more for the genuine. In Bottles: Ready to drink. Get Hires R.J. Root Beer wherever bottled beverages are sold, either by bottle or by the case. Healthful, economical. Make It At Home: For less than 1c a glass, it is easy to make 40 pint bottles of Hires R.J. Root Beer from one package of Hires Extract. A National Favorite. The Charles E. Hires Company, Philadelphia and Toronto."

Others soon began brewing their own root beer concoctions. In 1898, Edward Adolph Barq, Sr. bottled and began selling his root beer drink in Biloxi, Mississippi. The New Orleans-born Barq studied chemistry at the University of Paris, where he became fascinated with the way in which extracts and compounds interacted. This curiosity soon led to an interest in beverage-making. Returning to New Orleans in 1897, Barq took a job with a sugar refinery, though his heart's desire was still firmly locked on beverages. When the time was right, Barq launched a business in Biloxi, a place he considered a good location because of the high tourist trade. He and his wife washed bottles and filled them by hand from a single bottling line on Keller Avenue. Each morning they would load dozens of cases of their product on a horse-drawn wagon and visit local restaurants and soda fountain outlets. Though many of the drinks were citrus flavored, Barq's favorite, and the one he was continually trying to perfect, was root beer. It would be ten years before he achieved a formula that he felt was deserving of the slogan "Drink Barq's. It's Good."

In June, 1919, another root beer milestone was reached. World War One had just ended and America's troops were coming home. In Lodi, California, citizens lined the streets for an Armistice (now Veteran's) Day Parade. In the crowd was a man named Roy Allen who had brewed up a special toast for the returning soldiers, a drink made from roots, herbs and berries. He sold it, for a nickel a glass, to spectators and parade marchers who wanted to quench their thirst on that hot summer day. The drink was a hit and before long, Allen had opened three concession stands to sell his new drink. By 1922, Roy Allen had taken on Frank Wright as a partner and the two combined the first letters of their last names to create the first successful fast food chain, a business they called A&W. By 1950 there was a string of A&W root beer stands stretching from the coast to coast. A customer could drive in, park, and have a frosty mug of root beer delivered right to his car door. By 1971 A&W Root Beer was being bottled and sold at grocery and convenience stores nationwide. At the height of its popularity, there were 2400 A&W stands. Today there are believed to be about 550 in the US, and another 150 in various foreign countries.

Though the commercial foundations of root beer began to spread in the late 1800's and early 1900's, home brewed root beers had already been around for quite some time. In fact, as we have seen, using wild fruits, nuts, barks and roots to flavor drinks dates back thousands of years and is one of the oldest of the arts and crafts. The mysterious concoctions that were brought in to supplement the fruit-flavored sodas of the day had already been discovered - minus the carbonation - by nearly every farm wife and frontier cook. Remember, these were the people who had originally been given the recipes for sassafras and other teas by Native Americans.

Though they didn't have the benefit of carbonation, nor the ability to produce and distribute the drinks in quantity, they were already brewing tasty, thirst-quenching beverages for their own families from such ingredients as sassafras root, birch bark, burdock root, dandelion root, molasses, prickly ash bark, allspice, coriander, spikenard root, wild cherry bark, wintergreen, juniper berries and sarsaparilla. These homespun recipes were passed among family and friends and became quite widespread. The actual ingredients of the drinks varied, depending on who was doing the brewing, but the main ingredient always seemed to be sassafras.

Jim Dorsch, writer and staff member of CompuServe's Wine Forum, determined several root beer formulations based on materials obtained from the Siebel Institute in Chicago. The first recipe was for a drink made from oils of sassafras, betula (sweet birch), sweet orange, juniper berries and nutmeg. The second combined sassafras, wintergreen, peppermint, birch tar, and cinnamon. Another included wintergreen, sassafras, lemon, spruce, and nutmeg.

No one can say with absolute authority how many root beer brands have existed over the years. Tom Morrison, author of a book on root beer collectibles, has established positively the existence of 831 brands, based on evidence he has collected from bottles, cans, caps, and labels. Morrison speculates that this is far less than the actual number, which may be as high as two thousand! Nevertheless, between frontier homebrewers and the emerging commercial market, root beer established a firm foothold among beverages. Though other soft drinks would come to popularity, root beer held its position as a refreshing favorite.

A Celebration of America's Best-Loved Soft Drink

FROM SASSAFRAS TO SYNTHETICS: ROOT BEER INGREDIENTS

Throughout root beer's long and varied history, one fact has become clear: ingredients make the drink. Soda fountain proprietors knew this years ago when their customers began not only demanding something cold and sparkling in the glass, but something tasty, something that stimulated the palate and was different from anything else dispensed from the soda fountain's long pull-handles. This need for something that danced differently on the tongue was the reason root beer was born into popular culture, but the taste itself has had an attraction for quite some time.

The flavor that would eventually become the heart and soul of root beer was actually discovered somewhat by mistake, according to one popular story. When the Spanish arrived in Florida in 1565, they came across a tall fragrant tree with bright green oval-shaped leaves. They mistook it for the cinnamon tree, to which it bore a striking resemblance. The local Indians told them that, among other things, the bark of the root of this tree was highly effective in treating fever and rheumatism, and that they also used it as a blood purifier, a medical method that the Indians (and others) believed cured a great many ills.

An 1869 recipe for purification of the blood lists 4 ounces of sassafras root bark, 12 ounces of Honduras sarsaparilla, 6 ounces of guaiacum shavings, 4 ounces of wintergreen leaf, 4 ounces of elder flower, 3 ounces of yellow dock, 4 ounces of burdock root, 6 ounces of dandelion root, and 2 ounces of bittersweet root, all bruised. These were placed in a suitable pot, and one pint of alcohol was added, along with water sufficient to cover. After three to four days sitting in a moderately warm place, the recipe directed that one pint be poured off of the tincture and set aside until water was added to the ingredients and boiled to obtain the strength. "Pour off and add more water and boil again, then boil the two waters down to one quart, strain and add the liquor first poured off. Then add 2 & 1/2 pounds of crushed or coffee sugar and simmer to form a syrup." When cool, the mixture was bottled and sealed for later use. The dose was one to two tablespoons according to age and strength of the patient, given 1/2 hour before meals and at bedtime.

After some study, the Spanish began to realize that this wonder tree the Indians had been telling them so much about really wasn't the familiar cinnamon tree at all. Its shape, smell and taste were remarkably similar, but the tree itself was something different - another member of the Laurel family. In fact, they soon discovered that what the Indians were using as a virtual cure-all was the root bark of the Sassafras tree (Sassafras albidum).

Evidence of Sassafras root use is found in many cultures, but Native Americans were by far the biggest users of sassafras as a medical treatment. The Cherokee tribe which occupied Texas, northern Mexico, the Great Lakes Region, North and South Carolina, Tennessee, northern Georgia and Alabama were known to use sassafras as an antidiarrheal, antirheumatic, blood medicine, cold remedy, dermatological aid, dietary aid, eye medication, general disease remedy, pediatric aid and venereal aid. The Chippewa, who lived between Lake Huron and the Turtle Mountains in North Dakota, favored the root bark of the tree as a blood medicine, as did the Choctaw and the Delaware tribe of New Jersey, New York, Delaware and Pennsylvania.

The Iroquois Indians of the New York area liked sassafras as an anthelmintic (to eradicate intestinal worms), antirheumatic, blood medicine, dermatological aid, eye treatment, febrifuge (fever reducer), gynecological aid, hemostat (to control bleeding), hypotensive, orthopedic aid and tonic. The Koasati found sassafras to be helpful with heart problems and as a dermatological aid, while the Mohegans of Connecticut and New England used it as a tonic. Virginia's Rappahannock tribe used it to treat burns, as a dermatological aid, eye medication, febrifuge, and general disease remedy. Other tribes, including the Nanticoke and Houma also used sassafras in their medical treatments.

In 1575, Nicolas Monardes, the Spanish physician who was so interested in native plants, wrote a book detailing the astounding variety of medicinal plants being shipped to Europe by explorers and traders from the Western Hemisphere. Monardes raved about something he called the ague tree, which he described as one of the "great excellencies," used to heal "grievous and variable diseases." The Spanish, he wrote, were drinking the tea as a barrier and cure against malaria. In 1585, English settlers at Roanoke Island, near North Carolina, began to study the use of native plants. They discovered that sassafras was one of the few popular drugs growing wild. Not long after Monardes' book went to press, sassafras became a major export. Second only to tobacco, it became a staple of trade between the West and buyers in Europe. Unfortunately, sassafras soon gained a reputation as a cure for syphilis, an unjustified claim that soon cost the tree its respectability and popularity.

Though sassafras lost its fame commercially, to the Indians, settlers and explorers of North America it remained a sure-fire cure for many sicknesses. Sassafras root tea with cream and sugar added was claimed to be a muscle toner, astringent, and good for the skin. By adding a nip of goldenseal to the mixture, leg and foot swelling could be reduced. It was used as an analgesic, antiseptic, astringent, carminative (intestinal gas reliever), demulcent (skin soother), dentifrice, deputative (body waste cleanser), diaphoretic, diuretic, fungicide, insect repellent, pediculicide (to eliminate lice), rubefacient (to increase blood supply), stimulant, tea, viricide (to destroy viruses), mouthwash, perfume, sudorific (to encourage sweating), and tonic. It was also believed to help in the treatment of bronchitis, catarrh, colds, dysentery, eye problems, gout, kidney problems, disease, respiratory ailments, rheumatism, scurvy, skin infections, sores, swelling, syphilis, toothache, weaning, and hypertension. It was also popular as a massage agent.

Regardless of the medicinal claims, the bark of the roots were stripped, cut and pounded, mixed with water and boiled to produce an aromatic tea that became a favorite country drink. Passed from person to person, and then family to family, added to and improved upon, the sassafras tea recipe became a preferred backwoods refreshment. According to the popular legend, it stayed that way until Charles Hires tasted the blend at that rural New Jersey inn.

The tree is still fairly easily found. It is a native of the woods, fields and roadsides of eastern North America and can still be found flourishing from Ontario, south to Florida and Texas, and as far west as Michigan. Plant, herb and spice texts describe sassafras as an aromatic deciduous tree, averaging ten to forty feet tall (the largest sassafras tree on record is a 76-footer at Owensboro, Kentucky), with rough gray bark. Its bright green leaves are oval, with one to three lobes. From April through June greenish-yellow flowers appear and are followed by pea-sized fruits. But it is the bark covering the roots of the sassafras tree which is the key to the root beer taste. Though the branches, leaves, flowers and even the fruits were tried as flavorings, they failed to produce the same quality, resulting instead in a bitter, woody taste that made an almost undrinkable brew.

Through the years root beer manufacturers combined the oil distilled from boiling the sassafras root bark with other flavorings (some still used) to produce their own special brand of drinks. Allspice (Pimenta officinalis) was a favorite because its flavor was almost like a combination of cloves, nutmeg and cinnamon. The tree itself grows to approximately 30 feet, with thick leathery leaves and, in the summer, it bears dark, reddish-brown berries. The berries are picked when still green, then sun-dried and ground into powder. The wintergreen (Gaultheria procumbens) shrub, which grows to six feet tall, has creeping stems from which grow stalks that are topped by leathery, serrate leaves and whitish-pink flowers. Oil distilled from the leaves was used as a flavoring and is still popular today. Spikenard (Nardostachys jatamansi) was another common ingredient whose fragrant root was used, as was the root of sarsaparilla, a genus of American vine. Regardless of the natural ingredient combinations, the result was root beer, a drink that continued to rise in popularity.

In the early 1960's, however, a shakeup occurred that threatened the very existence of root beer. Long-term pharmacological studies in the laboratories of the United States Food and Drug Administration determined that a chemical compound called safrole (4-allyl-1,2-methylenedioxy-benzene $C_{10}H_{10}O_2$), the principal component of oil of sassafras, was a weak hepatic carcinogen, which causes cancer of the liver. The FDA's studies involved feeding substantial quantities of safrole to lab rats. The oral toxicity in these rats was found to be fifty percent lethality at a dose of 1.95 gram per kilogram. Though the small amount of safrole contained within a single bottle of root beer appears to be nowhere near even the bottom of the oral toxicity limit, the FDA decided to take no chances. Following a review of the data by scientists from both the government and the National Academy of Sciences, the FDA ruled that safrole, oil of sassafras, dihydrosafrole and iso-safrole (derivatives used as flavorings) were not be used as an additive in foods. 21 Code of Federal Regulations 189.180 makes it very clear: "Food containing any added safrole, oil of sassafras, isosafrole, or dihydrosafrole, as such, or food containing any safrole, oil of sassafras, iso-safrole, or dihydrosafrole, e.g., sassafras barks, which is intended solely or primarily as a vehicle for imparting such substances to another food, e.g., sassafras tea, is deemed to be adulterated in violation of the act based upon an order published in the Federal Register of December 3, 1960 (25 FR 12412)." By November 25, 1960, an extensive FDA survey of 3200 bottlers and suppliers disclosed that none of these substances were being used.

Soft drink companies who produced root beer using sassafras were forced to look elsewhere for a flavoring agent. The difficulty, not to mention the expense involved in attempting to remove the safrole from sassafras before using it as a food additive, forced most companies into devising artificial flavoring agents to replace the sassafras. And so the face and taste of root beer changed forever. Though the artificial flavoring used was, and continues to be, successful in sustaining the taste of the drink, the real heart of root beer was lost. If you have ever tasted real root-brewed root beer, you know what I mean. (Unfortunately, there aren't many people who can make this claim anymore.) Wintergreen is the modern substitute for sassafras, as well as vanilla and honey. Some brewers, like Barq's, use a version of sassafras extract with the safrole removed.

Today you can find sassafras bark, as well as sassafras extract (both with the safrole removed) and a powder called file (made from the leaves of the sassafras tree), in many health food or spice stores. Commercially, that is all that is available which comes close to real sassafras root. The root of the sassafras tree, the only part of the tree that really imparts the root beer flavor, is only found in the wild, mainly in the Eastern half of the United States. Its harvesting and use is highly discouraged and, for health reasons, should not be attempted.

Even if the FDA had not stepped in to alter the ingredients in root beer, technology and the changes in carbonated soft drink production likely would have done it for them sooner or later. Flavorings, sweeteners, colorings, acidulents, preservatives and artificially produced substitutes are common in soft drinks today, not to mention their use in a wide variety of food products. They are simply cheaper and more convenient to produce and use, and their use helps maintain freshness, preservation and taste in products that would otherwise have very short shelf lives.

Root beer was originally brewed for immediate use and country cooks made only enough for the family to drink. Preservation wasn't important because storage for long periods of time was practically unheard of. As root beer, and soft drinks in general, became popular, storing large batches became necessary. The soda fountain was devised to contain, carbonate and dispense soda waters. It worked well, but convenience was just then becoming an art form. Customers grew tired of trekking to the corner drugstore for a drink. They wanted their sodas at home where they could reach for a bottle anytime they grew thirsty. Before long, manufacturers began bottling individual drinks and selling them to grocery stores, markets and the general public. Today, soft drinks are manufactured and bottled for a standard shelf life of about six months. Their freshness depends on the preservatives, additives, acidulents, sweeteners and colorings used. These ingredients are specifically tailored to create and maintain the freshest, highest quality product possible.

Carbonated water is the leading ingredient in root beer and is listed first on the information label. The soft drink industry uses more than 10 billion gallons of water in soft drinks every year. All regular soft drinks contain 90% pure water, according to the National Soft Drink Association, and root beer is no exception. This water is filtered and specially treated in accordance with standard industry methods to remove any residual and local impurities, keeping the taste consistent from bottler to bottler. Because of this process the can of root beer you buy in Seattle will taste the same as a can of the same brand you purchase in Schenectady.

Flavorings are a vital ingredient in all soft drinks and manufacturers go to great lengths in combining them to create individual tastes. As we have seen, root beer was first made with raw sassafras root, a luxury that is no longer viable or legal for bottlers. Today, natural extracts, spices, herbs and oils can be used, along with chemically produced synthetic flavorings which combine to create that distinctive root beer taste. Each manufacturer creates their own unique combination and the actual ingredients that give a brand its special taste are usually listed only as "natural and artificial flavors" on the label. "There's no definition of what a root beer should be. It's almost like making a fruit punch," Phil Sprovieri, vice president of flavor extract company Flavorchem of Downers Grove, Illinois told the *Chicago Tribune.* "You can go spicy or you can make it smooth. Additives such as ginger add a little mystery to the potpourri of ingredients." Some of the possible flavorings are shown in the list we'll look at in a moment.

Another critical root beer ingredient is coloring. Though you would be hard-pressed to discern root beer from any other cola by sight alone, color has been proven to affect taste perception. Colorings can come from either natural or synthetic sources and provide that familiar light-to-dark brown appearance that we are so used to seeing in our mug. Caramel is a common root beer coloring agent.

Though soft drinks usually don't spoil because of their inherent acidity and added carbonation, storage conditions and storage time can have an affect on taste and flavor. Because of this, preservatives are used to prevent microbiological spoilage and chemical deterioration and maintain the quality of sodas. Acidulents also are used to preserve and to add a tartness to root beer. Some of the common preservatives and acidulents used in root beer are sodium benzoate and phosphoric acid.

Sweeteners are more than vital to root beer, and to all soft drinks for that matter. Without them, the liquid would be acidic and bland. Root beer is sweetened with either sucrose or High Fructose Corn Syrup (HFCS) made from corn, which are easily digestible and provide carbohydrates. Soft drinks generally contain anywhere from seven to fourteen percent sweetener. Diet soft drinks are slightly different, using low-calorie substitutes such as saccharin or aspartame (NutraSweet) to provide sweetness.

Carbon dioxide (CO_2), a colorless and odorless gas, is present in all carbonated beverages as an essential ingredient which gives sodas their characteristic refreshing fizz. When dissolved in water, CO_2 gives off a distinctive taste. Carbon dioxide is normally supplied to manufacturers as a solid (commonly known as dry ice) or a liquid maintained under high pressure in steel containers. Carbonation of the water or the finished drink is achieved by chilling the liquid and pouring it in slim layers over a series of plates in an enclosure containing CO_2 under pressure. As pressure is increased and temperature decreased, providing for precise absorption regulation, the gas is absorbed by the water.

The ingredients in root beer vary from brand to brand, but many are common no matter which bottle you're drinking from. All ingredients are listed on the label in order of decreasing amount. Here is a list of the commonly used ingredients, flavorings, colorings and additives available for use by root beer manufacturers today.

ALLSPICE OIL is a natural flavoring taken from the dried berries of the Allspice tree, a small West Indian tree of the Myrtle family. The tree has aromatic, shiny green leaves and white flowers. The oil of the berries is used to flavor root beer.

🍺 ALTHEA ROOT (Marshmallow Root) is a natural flavoring substance taken from a plant grown in Europe, Asia and the United States. It has tooth or heart-shaped leaves and light pink flowers. The dried root flavors root beer.

🍺 ANETHOLE is a colorless to slightly yellow liquid with a sweet taste and anise-like odor that is used as a flavoring agent in root beer and sarsaparilla. It is obtained from anise oil, fennel and other sources.

🍺 ANGELICA grows in Europe and Asia. An extract from this plant flavors root beer.

🍺 ANISE (Anise Seed, Star Anise) is the dried ripe fruit of the Anise bush, part of the Parsley family, which grows in Europe, Asia and the United States. The oil is a root beer flavoring. Anise belongs to the family Apiaceae and is classified as Pimpinella anisum.

🍺 ANISOLE is a synthetic agent used to flavor root beer.

🍺 ASPARTAME (NutraSweet) is a compound prepared from aspartic acid and phenylalanine. It is 200 times sweeter than sugar and is used to sweeten root beer.

🍺 BASIL EXTRACT (Sweet Basil) is an extract from the leaves and flowers of the herb Ocimum Basilicum. The oil flavors root beer.

🍺 BENZYL ALCOHOL is derived from pure alcohol and possesses a faintly sweet odor. It is used in synthetic root beer flavorings.

🍺 BIRCH SWEET OIL is from the bark of the birch tree (Betula lenta) and is used in root beer flavoring.

🍺 BLACKBERRY BARK EXTRACT is a natural flavoring agent extracted from the woody part of the Blackberry plant. It flavors root beer.

🍺 CARAMEL is used as a coloring and flavoring agent in root beer. It is produced by heating sugar or glucose and then adding a small amount of alkali or other trace mineral acid during the process.

🍺 CARBON DIOXIDE is a colorless, odorless, non-combustible gas used to carbonate root beer, as well as other soft drinks.

🍺 CARDAMOM OIL (also known as Grains of Paradise) is a natural flavoring and aromatic agent taken from the dried ripe seeds of native India, Ceylon and Guatemala plants. The seed oil is used to flavor root beer. The cardamom plant has large leaves and white flowers colored with blue stripes and yellow borders. The fruit is a small capsule with 8 to 16 brown seeds from which the oil is taken. Cardamom belongs to the family Zingiberaceae and is classified as Elettaria cardamomum.

- CASCARILLA BARK is from the Cascarilla tree growing in Haiti, the Bahamas and Cuba. The distilled oil is light yellow to amber with a spicy odor. It is used in root beer flavorings.

- CELERY SEED OIL is the yellowish to greenish-brown liquid distilled from the ripe fruit of the celery plant (family Apiaceae) grown in southern Europe. The oil is a flavoring in root beer.

- CHICORY EXTRACT is a natural root beer flavoring agent extracted from the chicory plant (family Asteraceae, classification Cichorium intybus). The plant has heads of large, bright blue flowers and the roots are much like that of the dandelion.

- CHINESE CASSIA BARK provides a natural flavoring extract. The oil distilled from the bark is used in root beer flavorings.

- CINNAMON BARK is the dried bark of cultivated cinnamon trees. It is one of the common flavorings found in root beer.

- CINNAMON LEAF OIL is the yellowish-brown volatile oil taken from the leaves and twigs of cinnamon trees. It is used to flavor root beer.

- CLARY (Clary Sage) is a natural extract of an aromatic herb that is grown in parts of southern Europe and England. Its oil is used in root beer flavorings.

- CLOVE BUD EXTRACT is a natural flavor from the strong, scented, reddish-brown dried flower buds of the tropical clove tree (family Myrtaceae, classification Syzygium aromaticum). The oil is derived from steam distillation of the dried stems and is used in root beer flavorings.

- CORIANDER OIL is a colorless or pale yellow oil taken from the dried seeds of the fruit of the Coriander plant (family Apiaceae, classification Coriandrum sativum) native to Asia and Europe. It is a root beer flavoring agent.

- CORN SYRUP (Dextrose) is a sweet syrup prepared from corn starch. It is used in root beer as a flavoring and may be described on packaging as High Fructose Corn Syrup.

- DANDELION ROOT AND LEAF (Tiger's Root) is obtained from the Taraxacum plant that grows throughout the United States. The root extract is used as a root beer flavoring.

- DIHYDROCOUMARIN is a synthetically produced root beer flavoring agent which is also found naturally in the Tonka bean, Oil of Lavender and Sweet Clover.

🍺 p-DIMETHOXYBENZENE is a synthetic root beer flavoring.

🍺 DIMETHYL POLYSILOXANE (Antifoam A) is an antifoaming agent used in soft drinks.

🍺 ESTRAGON (Tarragon) is a root beer flavoring taken from the oil of the leaves of the Tarragon plant (family Compositae, classification Artemisia dracunculus), which is native to Siberia and the regions near the Caspian Sea. The plant can reach a height of twenty four inches and produces small, green flowers.

🍺 ETHYL SALICYLATE (Salicylic Ether) is a synthetic flavoring agent used in root beer.

🍺 ETHYL VANILLIN are colorless flakes with an odor and flavor stronger than that produced by vanilla. It is used as a synthetic root beer flavoring.

🍺 EUCALYPTUS OIL (Dinkum Oil) is a colorless to pale yellow liquid derived from fresh Eucalyptus leaves. Used to flavor root beer.

🍺 FENNEL OIL is taken from the leaves and seeds of the Fennel plant (family Umbelliferae, classification Foeniculum vulgare). It is a root beer flavoring agent.

🍺 FENUGREEK (or Greek Hay) is an annual herb that grows in southern Europe, northern Africa and India. The leaves are described as triplicate leaflets that broaden toward the tip, with the middle leaflet sporting a stalk. The flowers are single, double, or triple, with a cylindrical seed pod. The seeds of fenugreek are ground and used as a root beer flavoring.

🍺 GENTIAN ROOT is the pale yellow, bitter tasting root of the perennial Gentian plant that grows in central and southern Europe. The oil flavors root beer.

🍺 GERANIOL is a synthetic root beer flavoring agent.

🍺 GINGER is from the root like stem of the ginger plant. An extract of it, as well as the oleoresin, is used in root beer flavoring

🍺 GUMACACIA (also listed as Acacia or Gum Arabic) is a tasteless, odorless, colorless dried exudate from the stem of the acacia tree which grows in Africa, India and the Near East, as well as in the United States. It is used in root beer primarily as a foam stabilizer.

🍺 HEMLOCK OIL (Spruce Oil) is a natural extract from the non-poisonous Hemlock tree native to North America and Asia. It is used as a root beer flavoring.

HOPS are an infrequent ingredient in root beer, but are occasionally used as a flavoring. Hops are derived from the dried fruit of the hop plant. Fresh hops are light yellowish or greenish and produce an oily liquid with a bitter taste and pungent odor. A solid extract of hops is sometimes used to flavor root beer.

HOREHOUND EXTRACT comes from the minty, bitter-tasting Horehound plant. The leaf surfaces of the plant contain tiny glands from which oil is obtained. The dried leaves and flowers are used to form an extract to flavor root beer.

ISOAMYL PYRUVATE is a colorless synthetic liquid used in root beer flavoring.

ISOBUTYL SALICYLATE is a colorless synthetic liquid used to flavor root beer.

JUNIPER is a North American, Europe and Asian tree whose dried ripe fruit provides a greenish-yellow extract and oil to flavor root beer.

KOLA NUT EXTRACT (Guru Nut) is naturally produced from the brown seed of the kola tree that grows in the West Indies, Africa and Brazil. It is a root beer flavoring.

LEMON is a common fruit from which an oil is derived from the fresh peel to flavor root beer.

LICORICE is a black substance obtained from the root of the licorice plant (Glycyrrhiza glabra). The substance, a colorless clucoside called glycyrrhizin, turns black in the process of extraction and is used as a flavoring for root beer.

LOCUST BEAN GUM is a natural extract from the seed of the Carob tree. It is used to flavor root beer.

MOLASSES EXTRACT is derived as a byproduct of the processing of cane sugar and is a natural root beer flavoring.

NUTMEG is the dried ripe seed of the Nutmeg tree (family Yristicaceae) used in root beer flavorings.

OCOTEA CYMBARUM OIL is obtained from the distillation of the wood of a tree common to Brazil. It is used as a sassafras oil substitute.

OREGANO (Origanum Oil) is found throughout Eurasia and is spicier than the majoram plant, which is similar. The extracted oil is used to flavor root beer.

- PHOSPHORIC ACID (H3PO4) is a colorless and odorless liquid made by treating calcium phosphate rock with sulfuric acid and then filtering the resulting liquid to remove the calcium sulfate. It is used as an acidulent and flavoring in soft drinks.

- PIPSISSEWA LEAVES EXTRACT is taken from the leaves of a Cree (Indian)-named evergreen shrub and is used to flavor root beer.

- POTASSIUM SORBATE (Sorbic Acid) is a white powder used as a preservative and fungistat in beverages.

- PRICKLY ASH BARK is the bark taken from the Prickly Ash tree and used to flavor root beer.

- p-PROPYL ANISOLE is a synthetic flavoring agent with a distinct anise odor. Used to flavor root beer.

- QUASSIA EXTRACT (Bitter Ash) is an alkaloid obtained from the wood of the Quassia amara tree native to South America, Jamaica and the Caribbean Islands. Used to flavor root beer.

- QUILLAIA (Soap Bark, China Bark, Panama Bark) is an extract of the inner dried bark of Quillaja saponara, a South American tree. It is used as a root beer flavoring agent.

- SACCHARIN is an artificial sweetener used since 1879. It is three hundred times sweeter than sugar and is generally odorless. In 1977 the FDA announced that it planned to ban the use of saccharin in food and soft drinks because a Canadian government study found that it caused malignant bladder tumors in laboratory animals. The FDA delayed the ban due to complaints from commercial producers and users. It is still considered hazardous to health and may be a cancer-causing agent in humans.

- SARSAPARILLA EXTRACT is the dried root of the sarsaparilla plant and is commonly used to flavor root beer.

- SASSAFRAS BARK EXTRACT is the yellow to reddish-yellow oil of the root of the sassafras tree (family Lauraceae, classification Sassafras albidum) with the safrole removed. Though the oil of the root bark is banned, this extract, usually made by passing alcohol or an alcohol-water mixture through the oil, is free of the carcinogen safrole. It is a root beer flavoring.

- SNAKEROOT OIL, obtained from the Snakeroot plant (family Polygalaceae), is native to Canada and parts of the United States. It is a natural root beer flavoring agent.

- **SODIUM BENZOATE** is a white, odorless substance in either powder or crystal form which has a sweet, slightly antiseptic taste. It is used as a preservative in root beer.
- **SORBIC ACID** is a white powder derived from the berries of the Mountain Ash. It is a mold and yeast inhibitor sometimes used in soft drinks.
- **WINTERGREEN OIL** (Menthyl Salicylate) is obtained naturally by distillation from the betula, teaberry oil or sweet birch shrubs. The extract is used as a root beer flavoring.
- **YEAST** is a fungus used to convert sugar to alcohol or carbon dioxide. It is often used by home brewers to carbonate root beer.
- **ZINGERONE** occurs naturally in ginger and is a synthetic flavoring sometimes included in root beer.

Root beer, like any other soft drink, is created and packaged in a basic six step process. First, water is super-purified and filtered. Second, a syrup base is created from the flavorings, sweeteners, colorings, etc., and added to the water. Then a carbonater machine adds carbon dioxide. Next, the liquid is transferred under pressure to a filling machine which fills individual bottles or cans and the containers are immediately sealed. In step five the containers are sprayed with warm water to bring them to room temperature and prevent condensation, and then dried. Finally, labels are added if they have not been pre-printed on the containers. The modern bottling plant often produces soft drinks under contract to a franchise company which provides them with the flavor concentrates or beverage bases from which the final product is created. The average major bottlers' production line can churn out more than two thousand containers per minute.

Along with the ingredients panel on root beer containers is the now-familiar Nutrition Facts label, which the US Food and Drug Administration has required on all food packaging since 1994. This panel lists serving size (sometimes abbreviated "Serv. size"), the amount customarily consumed by a person at one time (normally 8 fluid ounces - 240 mL) for root beer and most soft drinks, and servings per container, denoting the amount of servings available in each container. But the panel also lists important dietary and nutritional information that we all should bear in mind when we hoist a can.

Of particular interest is the amount of calories in root beer. Calories are a unit of measure that express the energy-producing value of foods and drinks. The values printed on the nutrition label of root beer containers are based on a two-thousand calorie daily diet. As an example, a 12-ounce can of A&W Root Beer contains 170 calories, while 12-ounces of Mug Root Beer has 160 calories. Carbohydrates, a little-understood, but always listed value, are composed mainly of sugar, starch, dextrin, and cellulose. In soft drinks, sugars and organic acids make up the bulk of the carbohydrate value. Using our examples of A&W and Mug, we find 44 grams and 43 grams respectively. The total fat in root beer, expressed in grams, is usually zero. Sugar, on the other hand, is a popular sweetener for root beer and other soft drinks and weighs in at a higher number: 44 grams in A&W, 43 in Mug. Sodium in root beer normally comes from the carbonated water used and generally is very low: 55 grams in A&W, 65 in Mug. In fact, many root beers advertise themselves as "low sodium" (less than 140 mg per serving) or "very low sodium" (less than 35 mg per serving). Protein, the last listing on the nutrition label, is commonly zero for root beer.

TASTE TESTS: WHICH ROOT BEER IS BEST?

In the mid-1970's, the Pepsi-Cola Company launched an advertising campaign that would go down in marketing history. They called it the Pepsi Challenge, a series of blind taste tests that asked consumers to try Pepsi and Coca-Cola and "let your taste decide" which was better. Pepsi claimed that more people nationwide preferred their drink over Coke. The tests were soon turned into television commercials, showing millions that there was a difference between the two drinks and you could taste it. If the Pepsi Challenge did anything beyond selling more of that company's product, it certainly proved that when it comes to soft drinks, taste is paramount.

But, what about root beer? There hasn't been a "Hires Challenge" to get us thinking about root beer taste. And anyway, isn't one root beer really just like the other? Can we honestly say that Hires is very much different from Ramblin'? That Barq's is distinctive from A&W? There was a time when I believed - back in the days when it was just my favorite drink and not something to be analyzed and written about - that one root beer was like any other. You popped the top, heard that wonderful hiss of escaping fizz, and drank. I hate to say it now, it's almost sacrilege to admit it, but I cared little what kind of root beer I drank, and usually bought whatever was cheapest or available at the time. If it was root beer it was good enough for me.

However, when I began to research and then write this book, things changed. It wasn't a subtle change or a gradual transfiguration, it was an overwhelming, slam-bang, in-your-face revelation! In a matter of days my world view switched and I began buying root beer, drinking root beer, making root beer, and basically living the entire root beer experience. All other soft drinks were forsaken; banished from my sight. The mere mention of a non-root beer drink was frowned on if not verboten. Wherever I went I ordered root beer, whenever I went shopping I bought root beer. There was root beer in my refrigerator, root beer in my closets, root beer everywhere! It was total immersion and it drove everyone around me crazy. Friends and family started saying root beer like it was a dirty word, using it with derision and adding with a laugh: "Oh, she's writing that book on root beer."

Fortunately, all of this study, in-depth investigation and single-minded dedication paid off. Before the last word was typed, I had formed very definite opinions about root beer, the different brands and what exactly makes a root beer good. These opinions are totally my own views and are undoubtedly tainted by one too many bottles of Henry Weinhard's and cans of Barq's. So, I encourage you to go out and do your own taste tests. Don't rely on my two cents, it's certainly not the last word. You are sure to come to different conclusions and I invite you to write and tell me about them.

Rating root beer is like rating the density of fog: it's shadowy, elusive and constantly changing. At first I wasn't sure you could place any kind of standards on root beer taste. I sipped a bit of that one, a touch of this one and I tried to pick out the differences. Just what is it that makes a root beer good? What is it that makes this one taste different from that one? The answer is as different - and confusing - as each person you ask. Eventually I found that four standards can be used to rate root beer: Flavor, Texture, Aftertaste, and Carbonation/Foam.

Flavor is the big one, the leading indicator of taste. It's what you first discern as the liquid hits your tongue and it's what will keep you drinking until the can is empty. Every manufacturer's ultimate goal is to create a distinctive and delicious flavor that will send his product flying off the shelves and into consumers' refrigerators.

Texture is not immediately apparent, but it's what you taste if you allow a sip of root beer to float around in your mouth for fifteen seconds or so. It's the second component of flavor and it's difficult to describe, but you'll definitely know it when you taste it.

Aftertaste is probably my number one pet peeve about root beer. A root beer that is done right leaves a pleasant, refreshing tang on the tongue long after the liquid is gone. Unfortunately, the artificial ingredients in many root beers force a kind of sickly-sweet metallic aftertaste that makes you want to wash it away with a cold glass of water. Aftertaste is vital, because if it's pleasant it will bring you back for more, and if it's not, the rest of the drink may end up being poured down the drain.

The carbonation/foam factor might seem unimportant at first blush, sort of the novelty aspect of root beer, but it's actually quite significant. If you've ever tasted flat root beer (and who hasn't?) you know what I mean. All root beers fizz when you pop the top, as the carbon dioxide that has been trapped within escapes, but it's what happens after that that counts. To test the carbonation/foam factor of a root beer, open a new can and immediately pour it into a tall glass. A good root beer builds a strong head of foam and even after the foam has diminished, you can still see tiny bubbles of carbonation popping off the surface of the drink. If you don't see them, you'll feel them invade your nose when you tip the glass back for a sip. Carbonation that lasts a few hours is the sure sign of a winner.

In the beginning, when you are studying root beer, every brand is new and every taste is unique. I began my investigation by buying a six-pack of A&W, Barq's, Dad's and Hires, brands that were available nearly everywhere and that seemed to be well liked. Later I added others like Albertson's A+, Arizona Root Beer Float, Hansen's, Henry Weinhard's, IBC, Mug, President's Choice, Sam's Choice and Stewart's. The criteria for testing were fairly simple: the root beer had to be widely available and it had to be something I could easily obtain. These comments are therefore limited to the thirteen brands listed above. A real taste test, of course, would involve a a lot more people, many more brands, and be much more scientific. My tests are hardly scientific, but they'll give you an idea of what to look for in your own selections. If you're a root beer manufacturer and would like your brand tested and reviewed for the next edition of this book, please contact the publisher.

A&W. Mr. A and Mr. W sure knew what they were doing when they brewed up their first batch of this root beer. It has a sharp flavor and a pleasant texture, along with an aftertaste that doesn't overwhelm you. Carbonation is long-lasting, though the foam factor is marginal.

Albertson's A+. Distributed exclusively by Albertson's grocery stores, this root beer was a bit disappointing. It has a slightly medicinal hint to its flavor which affects the texture and lasts well into the aftertaste. Carbonation is good, though it failed to foam up to standards. A mediocre showing.

🍺 *Arizona Root Beer Float.* If you like it when the ice cream in your root beer float melts, then this drink is for you. The only root beer I could find that includes milk and cream, this drink's flavor is overpowered by those two ingredients, killing the texture and leaving a milky aftertaste. Not my favorite, but float fans will go crazy over it.

🍺 *Barq's.* This Barq's has a bite. The flavor is distinctive and sharp, though slightly acidic, with a texture that packs a heck of a bite. Rumor has it that the bite comes from cinnamon, but I've been unable to confirm it. Carbonation is on target, but the foam factor is disappointing.

🍺 *Dad's.* An old favorite, this drink has a flavor that is slightly too sweet, but still doesn't fail to satisfy. The texture falls off quickly, to end in an aftertaste that mirrors the flavor. Carbonation is good. Overall, if you like your root beer good and sweet, this is the one.

🍺 *Hansen's.* This is the only root beer I've ever come across that is clear. If you close your eyes, you won't even notice. The flavor is keen, not too sweet, with a texture that blends right in. It's different, with a cinnamon-honey-ginger type of taste that I found to be a neat change. Carbonation held up, even after sitting in a warm car for an hour, but the foam made a nearly non-existent showing.

🍺 *Henry Weinhard's.* The Blitz-Weinhard people are known for their beers, but they have made a big showing in the soft drink market with this root beer. The flavor is characteristic of old time root beers, with a strong taste backed by a creamy vanilla-honey flavoring. The texture is remarkable; soft yet tasty. The aftertaste is equally as soft. Carbonation is good, though it tends to fall off quickly once the bottle is opened. The foam is the best of any root beer I've tried and it just lasts and lasts. An excellent showing.

🍺 *Hires.* The first commercially produced root beer is still a strong contender. The Hires flavor is a good balance, not overly sweet, with a positive texture. The aftertaste is pleasant. Carbonation is good, with a solid foam factor. A great showing.

🍺 *IBC.* One of the few that still comes in bottles, this root beer holds its own, with a flavor that may be too sweet for some. Nevertheless, the texture is strong and clear, and the aftertaste passable. Carbonation is good, but the foam is something you have to search for. A good showing.

- *Mug.* A pleasantly flavored root beer with a solid texture, Mug's sweet aftertaste doesn't take away from it. Carbonation is superb, but the foam doesn't last long enough. A great showing.

- *President's Choice.* Another brand created for a grocery store, this one stands right up with the better known name brands. It has a good, stable flavor and texture, with an aftertaste only slightly too sweet. Carbonation is good, with a mediocre foam factor. A good showing.

- *Sam's Choice.* Yet another supermarket brand, Sam's Choice is sold through Wal-Mart stores nationwide. It has a disappointing flavor, with a slightly acidic texture. The aftertaste is sweet, but carbonation is good. An average showing.

- *Stewart's.* One of the bottled root beer brands, with a sweet flavor and a texture that is covered a bit by the carbonation. The aftertaste is pleasant and carbonation is strong. A good showing. This brand has depth.

This quick survey illustrates that no two root beers are created equal, especially when considered side by side. Flavor is highly dependent on a manufacturer's choice of ingredients and the amounts of those ingredients. A brewer who includes sassafras extract, vanilla, honey and cinnamon is going to produce a vastly different drink than one who does without these ingredients. A high corn syrup content is going to overpower the root beer taste and produce a drink that is more sweet than anything else.

So is there a best root beer? You can decide for yourself in your own quest for the best. I recommend you try any and every brand you can locate. As they say, the journey is the reward!

A Celebration of America's Best-Loved Soft Drink

BASEMENT BREWING: MAKING YOUR OWN ROOT BEER

In the world of root beer production there are three distinct levels: major manufacturer, independent microbrewer and homebrewer. We have dissected the first and taken a peek at the second. Now let's consider homebrewing, which both predates and antedates modern root beer. Though other producers of the drink will rise and fall, swell and fade away, the homebrewer will always exist and persist. After all, root beer didn't begin in a manufacturing plant with massive rolling production lines, it began in iron kettles in country kitchens and frontier encampments. No matter what modern manufacturers do to this drink, no matter how many artificial ingredients are used or how many different commercial brands are created in response to a real or perceived need, root beer's heritage is solid. It began with home brewers and it continues as a favorite homebrew drink. The number of people brewing root beer in their kitchens and basements these days would surprise you. It's one part hobby, one part tradition, and another part sheer fun. And you can join in, too.

The great thing about brewing root beer is that anyone can do it. In fact, it's an amazingly uncomplicated process, as I learned when I sat down to make my first batch. I was surprised that there wasn't more to it and I worried that I had done something wrong, missed some vital ingredient. I was sure that when I cracked the top on the first bottle I would have some undrinkable, disease-laden horror that needed to be poured down the drain before it launched a major epidemic! My fears were groundless and the results of my brewing weren't half bad.

Root beer is simply water that has been sweetened, flavored and carbonated. The major manufacturers, like Hires or A&W, have streamlined the combining process and have added some other ingredients to preserve and protect their drinks, but they all share the basic ingredients: water, sweetener, flavoring, and carbonation. You and I can combine the same ingredients to produce nearly the same drinks. Sure, the majors have special flavorings that they add to give their drinks a distinctive taste, but other than that, the process is the same. Let's look at the ingredients one by one.

Water is universal, you'll find it anywhere and everywhere. It is fundamental to life as we know it and it's the main ingredient in root beer. But, do we just want to turn on the tap to supply the water for our homebrewing? Yes and no. Tap water is "OK" for brewing root beer. The major problem with tap water, however, is that it contains chlorine, fluoride, sulfates, minerals and various and sundry other microscopic entities. Each of these contribute to the overall taste of tap water and hence, the taste of your root beer. The major suppliers of soft drinks treat and filter their water before use, removing impurities and assuring that the water meets their standards. You and I, however, don't have access to our own water filtration plants, so we're left with having to look for alternate methods.

Your local water district maintains a statistical breakdown of your tap water content and will provide you with a copy of the latest analysis if you ask them nicely. Most of the technical mumbo-jumbo on the report will be undiscipherable to all but a trained microbiologist, but with a little study you should be able to determine the basic content. Beer home brewers, who have to worry about the content of water much more than root beer brewers do, have several guidelines that are helpful:

pH-Neutral - A high pH with high hardness levels is undesirable.

Chlorine - Should not be present, or at least present in very small quantities.

Calcium - Desirable, in a concentration between 50-100 ppm.

Sulfate (SO_4 -2) - Contributes to bitterness. Desired concentration is below 450 ppm.

Magnesium ($Mg+2$) - Too much can cause a sour, bitter or salty taste. Concentration should be less than 30 ppm.

Chloride ($Cl-1$) - Less than 200-250 ppm.

Sodium ($Na+1$) - Desirable levels are 70-150 ppm.

Carbonate (CO_3 -2) - Concentrations should be less than 50 ppm.

Bicarbonates (2(HCO3 -2)) - Concentrations should be less than 25 ppm, definitely not over 100.

Hardness - low hardness (less than 50 ppm) is good.

Iron - Concentrations should be less than 0.5 ppm

Zinc - Concentrations should be less than 0.2 ppm

Manganese - Concentrations should be less than 0.2 ppm

I can almost guarantee that your water content breakdown is not going to match these ideal concentration levels. Luckily, as root beer home brewers, we don't have to worry too much about the quality of our water. If you decide to use tap water - and many do because it's so accessible, consider attaching a good quality filter to your faucet. Not only is this good for your health, but it will certainly improve the taste of your water and hence your root beer. An alternative to tap water is bottled or mineral water. You can purchase this at your grocery store, in just about any size container. Most bottled water is already treated and filtered, saving you the hassle. For our purposes, any type of non-carbonated water will do.

Sweetener is next on the list of ingredients and you won't have to go far to find it, either. For the homebrewer, pure granulated sugar is the sweetener of choice. Not only is it by far the most cost effective, it also can be easily fermented by yeast to provide natural carbonation. Other ingredients which can be used to sweeten root beer are molasses, fructose, corn sugar, brown sugar, raw cane sugar, Aspartame (NutraSweet) and Sweet-N-Low. I would suggest that you make your first batch of root beer with pure granulated sugar and leave the other possibilities for later experimentation.

Flavoring is perhaps the most talked about aspect of root beer brewing. After all, flavoring is the be all and end all of your drink. Without flavoring all you have is sweet, carbonated water and we all know how appealing that is! There are two ways to flavor your homebrewed root beer; the easy way and the hard way. Let's try doing it the easy way first. Most homebrew beer equipment stores and many herb and spice specialty shops sell root beer extract. You may also stumble across such an extract in your grocery store's baking aisle, though it seems to be rare these days. The extract is simply a concentrated flavoring, containing many of the same artificial colorings and flavorings as commercially sold root beer. Many years ago, Charles Hires sold packets of solid extract that could be mixed with water to create Hires Root Beer. Though the Hires Company no longer sells their extract, other companies sell their own versions of root beer flavoring. Extracts are the easiest way to get flavoring into your root beer without too much mess and hassle. One bottle usually provides enough to make four to five gallons of root beer. You can, however, choose to do things the hard way.

As we've discussed, the real flavor of root beer comes from the sassafras root bark and other natural ingredients such as allspice, birch bark, ginger and spikenard. With a little patience and persistence, you may be able to find all or most of these ingredients in health food stores or herb and spice stores. Sassafras root bark will probably be hardest to find, though I did stumble across it in a Boney's Health Food Market. It carried a prominent warning "not to be used for human consumption." The actual procedure for making root beer from these ingredients is outlined in the recipes section later in this book. The basic method involves washing, chopping (optional) and boiling the roots for thirty minutes, at which time the sweetener, additional water and yeast is added. If you choose to use real ingredients, I urge you to be *extremely careful* in making sure that what you buy is suitable for consumption. There's no telling what you may find in the racks and bins at health food shops, so ask first and be sure to tell them what you're going to use the ingredient for.

Carbonation is the bane of any homebrewer and for those of us pursuing the perfect root beer, it's a subject that will be hashed and rehashed. The big boys like Barq's and Hires inject carbon dioxide (CO2) into their mixtures with professional carbonating equipment. You and I, however, have to make do with a method that's a bit more difficult and time-consuming, but yields nearly the same results. Instead of CO2, homebrewed root beer is carbonated naturally through the actions of yeast. Yeast is a microscopic-sized, one-celled fungi that is probably quite familiar to you. It has been used for thousands of years in the making of wine and bread, and is also used in the making of other foods and in the production of some antibiotics and hormones. Yeast can ferment carbohydrates in certain substances, and that little trick of nature comes in quite handy for making our root beer fizz. When we add yeast to root beer, it immediately goes to work feasting on the sugar in the mixture. The result of this feeding frenzy is the production of carbon dioxide, or in soda terms, carbonation. The amount of time it takes to ferment varies with the potency of the yeast, plus the temperature of the mixture and the outside air. More about that in a minute, when I walk you through a root beer making session. You can pick up packets of champagne, wine or beer yeast from a homebrew beer store, or Red Star or Fleischman's from your local grocery store. Some people claim that bread yeast imparts a yeasty taste to the drink and shouldn't be used, but I haven't found this to be a problem. By the way, you can also go an easier route by adding carbonated mineral or seltzer water to your mixture, bypassing the yeast process altogether. It's easier and it tastes just as good, but it isn't half as much fun!

So, enough theory. Let's go into the kitchen and get the pots bubbling. The first order of business is to find something to bottle up all this root beer you're about to make. There's nothing like having a nice batch ready and nothing to pour it into. Purists will insist that you buy glass bottles along with crown caps and a bottle-capper machine. These may look nice, but they are not necessary. All you really need are one-liter plastic soda bottles with their original screw cap lids. Wash them out thoroughly with hot water and soap; dish washing detergent works fine, as does a small amount of bleach. Pay special attention to the little nooks and crannies at the bottom of the bottles. This cleaning process is doubly important if you've had the bottles sitting out in the sun waiting to be recycled. Any odd fungal growth may be dangerous to you, as well as imparting a nasty taste to your root beer. If you really want to get serious about sterilization, homebrew stores will sell you sulfite crystals which can be mixed with water to create a solution for washing bottles. The only difficulty with this is that you must ensure that the solution is completely flushed from the bottles before use or you'll encounter a surprising and unwelcome taste to your root beer. Once you have several clean liter bottles ready to go, it's time to set up the kitchen.

You will need a measuring cup, a container large enough to mix everything in (12 cups or larger should do the trick), and a mixing spoon. And it doesn't hurt to wear an apron, either, just in case the extract gets away from you. You'll also need one packet of yeast, warm water, 1 tablespoon (1/2 ounce) of root beer extract and two cups of sugar. Let's start by making one gallon of root beer, just to get the hang of things.

 You will need 1/8 to 1/4 of a tablespoon of yeast.

 Add this to one cup of warm water (lukewarm to the touch, not hot, not cold) and let it stand for five minutes. This is the most critical part of the entire process, as the yeast must dissolve completely. If, after five minutes or more, the yeast is not dissolved, throw away the mixture, break open another packet and try again.

- Next, combine one tablespoon of root beer extract and two cups of sugar in a bowl of warm water. How much water? Enough to dissolve the sugar in. Stir it well until most of the sugar is dissolved, then add the yeast mixture.

- To this add enough warm water to bring the entire mixture to the one gallon level. It's best to use a one gallon bowl, otherwise you'll end up estimating.

- At this point you can dip a spoon into your mixture and taste it. Not sweet enough? Add more sugar. Not enough root beer taste? Add a bit more extract. Your taste buds will tell you when it's right.

- Now, fill your liter bottle to within one inch of the top and twist on the cap tightly. If you measured incorrectly and you have more mixture left over, just use another bottle. Remember that the cap should be sealed tightly to ensure good carbonation.

- Set the bottles aside for three to four days at room temperature. Don't put them in the sun, next to a stove or microwave or near the refrigerator.

- After three or four days, move your bottles to a cool, dark place (a cabinet works fine) and allow them to stand for one to two weeks.

The yeast needs time to do its thing, and some yeast takes longer than others, so the actual time may vary. It is critical that you check the bottles daily by gently squeezing them. When they are firm, they're ready. If you used glass bottles, you'll need to crack the cap and check for the sound of escaping air. The degree of carbonation is harder to check if you're using glass bottles, so I recommend the plastic type. Once the bottles are firm to the touch, carbonation is complete. Refrigerate the bottles to stop the process. It is possible for fermenting bottles to explode or otherwise overflow if the fermentation process is allowed to continue too long or the bottle caps are not applied tightly. For this reason, keep a close eye on your bottles. Check them daily.

After fermentation it is quite normal to find a layer of yeast taking up residence at the bottom of your bottles. These yeastie beasties have worked hard carbonating your root beer. Just pour carefully and the deposit should remain on the bottom. When the bottle is empty, be sure to rinse out the bottom well, using a bottle brush if necessary to clean it completely. You can also decant the liquid into another container, then reseal and refrigerate.

A Celebration of America's Best-Loved Soft Drink

ROOT BEER INGREDIENTS TABLE

(Amounts may vary depending on extract used, consult extract bottle)

AMOUNT	YEAST	EXTRACT	SUGAR	WATER
1 Gallon	1/8-1/4 tsp	1 Tbs.	2 cups	Fill to 1 gallon
2 Gallons	1/4-1/2 tsp	1 oz.	4 cups	Fill to 2 gallons
4 Gallons	1/2-1 tsp	1 bottle	8 cups	Fill to 4 gallons

That's the procedure in a nutshell. There are almost infinite variations, but this is the easiest and seems to work the best, especially for beginners. An even simpler version makes about two to six cups of non-carbonated root beer. Use 1/4 tablespoon of root beer extract to 12 ounces of water, and stir in two tablespoons of sugar or other sweetener. It tastes just as good, but you'll miss the fizzies.

Any problems encountered while brewing root beer usually have to do with yeast. Yeast can be affected by several things. If it is old, stale or has been left open it will likely fail to dissolve thoroughly enough for proper carbonation to take place. Always make sure you're using fresh yeast. If the yeast doesn't dissolve properly, throw it away and start again. The amount of yeast you use will directly affect carbonation. Too little yeast will yield low or nonexistent carbonation, while too much will over-carbonate and possibly cause exploding bottles. Generally, for one gallon of root beer use 1/8 to 1/4 tablespoon of yeast, for two gallons use 1/4 to 1/2 tablespoon and for four gallons use one half to 1 tablespoon.

Water temperature also has a great deal to do with yeast development. Dissolve the yeast in a cup of lukewarm water (98-110 F). Water that is too hot will kill the yeast, water that is too cold will not activate the yeast. It's a delicate balance, but it truly isn't as hard as it sounds. With a little practice, you'll get the hang of it.

All home brewers have initial concerns about exploding bottles and root beer brewers are no exception. If you use glass bottles, your chances of encountering a geyser are higher than if you use plastic bottles. This is simply because it is more difficult to check carbonation levels with a glass bottle. Once you have your recipe and fermentation time down to a near-science, you'll be able to use glass bottles with more confidence. I recommend using plastic soda bottles as they are much easier to check and the danger level is lower in the event one of them explodes. For safety's sake, make sure that the caps are tight. Again, store your bottles in a cabinet or closet away from any hot spots such as microwaves, water heaters, etc. Check the carbonation level daily by gently squeezing the sides of the bottles. A good way to determine the carbonation is to squeeze a store-bought bottle of soda. Notice that it's as hard as a rock? That's just about what you're striving for. Once the bottles are firm, they're ready. Refrigerate them immediately. I once brewed up four bottles of root beer, stored them in a cabinet for a week, and only checked them once. When I finally got around to feeling the bottles they were harder than granite and one of them was distorted from the pressure. I placed them in a sink and one by one gently cracked the caps, letting the gases escape. It was touch and go for awhile, but luckily nothing exploded. This illustrates the potential dangers when dealing with carbonation. Always keep a close eye on things and make sure your bottles are stored where children can't reach them.

One concern of new root beer brewers is the alcohol content of naturally carbonated root beer. It's true that the yeast fermentation process does produce a small amount of alcohol but the total is negligible (less than 1%), and is not considered to be intoxicating.

Now that you have brewed up your first batch of root beer, why not create your own personalized labels for your bottles? Shane Patton, who maintains an Internet World Wide Web page devoted to root beer, makes his own labels. First, he designs the labels using a graphics program on his computer and prints them out on a laser printer. Then he carefully cuts the labels out and trims them. Next he fills a saucer with milk and lays the label face up on the surface of the milk. After about five seconds he lifts the label out and places it on the bottle, pressing firmly. The last step is to dry any milk from the sides of the label. "You may be thinking 'milk?' - but really, it does work," says Patton. "The sides won't peel off and there's no tape or gluey mess to deal with. I myself was skeptical, but was amazed with the results. Apparently it is the lactose in the milk that gives it its adhesive quality."

DRIPS AND DROPS: ROOT BEER AS A HOBBY

If you thought the root beer experience ended with the drink itself you're in for quite a surprise. A frosty mug on a hot afternoon may be sufficient for you, but for many, root beer has evolved into much more than just a soft drink. People all over the world collect root beer memorabilia, create and maintain Internet World Wide Web sites devoted to the topic, participate in Internet newsgroup discussions and more. Believe it or not, an entire hobby has sprung up around the drink. If it has to do with root beer, it's considered fair game.

The hobby of collecting is probably as old as the Stone Age, when primitive man (or woman) found a pretty rock and decided to keep it. Over the years, people have collected everything and anything you can think of, creating in the process sometimes massive assortments of objects. In the world of root beer, collectibles are a big thing. Collectors worldwide hunt for root beer memorabilia that ranges from new brands, to cans, bottles, labels, advertisements, promotional items, books and more. But by far the largest part of root beer collecting focuses on bottles.

Dave Nader, a Wisconsin collector and editor of the monthly *Root Beer Float* newsletter, said that "primitive" pottery and stoneware root beer bottles, as well as transfer type and Applied Color Label bottles are popular collector's items. Nader defines primitive-style pottery and stoneware bottles as "those pottery bottles that are debossed, incised or known to be of an older nature." Don Yates, author of *American Stone Ginger Beer and Root Beer Bottles*, categorizes primitives as bottles of the 1780-1880 era. "Many of the primitives were handmade on potter's wheels or hand pressed; they had the owner's name impressed in the soft clay prior to firing in the kiln." Transfer-type bottles, on the other hand, are those where the information on the bottle is not embossed, or debossed, but is actually printed on the bottle with an ink, according to Nader. Don Yates explains that transfer type bottles, usually of the 1880-1920 era, were stamped with an ink pattern and then coated with a Bristol glaze prior to firing.

Applied Color Label or ACL bottles, another popular collector's item, have a color label applied on them. Several lesser known categories also exist: embossed glass bottles, paper label bottles, and extract bottles. Collectors often specialize, concentrating on one category of particular interest, but it isn't uncommon to find a collector who likes to acquire a little bit of everything.

Looking at the long and rich history of root beer, it isn't difficult to see why collecting this type of memorabilia is so popular. What true root beer aficionado wouldn't love to own an original bottle of Hires extract from the 1800's? Or one of the first A&W mugs with the now famous bullseye and arrow? How about a Dad's Root Beer disposable miniature flashlight or an A&W thermometer? Of course, it doesn't have to be vintage to be collectible. I discovered three different models of Dad's Root Beer pocket watches being sold at a local Target department store. They're probably not worth much in the collectibles market because of the easy availability, but in several years who knows? They may be a hot item. As may be expected, the older and harder an item is to come by, the more it should be worth. And, of course, price is a highly variable point; one collector may pay more for something that he just has to have for his collection than another person will. It's the law of supply and demand. The ongoing root beer wars between manufacturers are also expected to cause an increase in the demand, and hence the value, of root beer collectibles.

Rule #1 for root beer collecting, according to Dave Nader, is buy only what you like. That's the entire idea behind collecting: you acquire something because you like it, not because you think it may be worth something someday. Rule #2 is to always strive to buy quality. "Don't confuse cheap with quality," said Nader. "Quality refers to condition, in this case. Condition should be as near to mint as possible. Experience will eventually tell you when it is time to deviate from this rule." Rule #3 is almost obvious: plan on making mistakes. "You will eventually pay too much for something, usually by finding it cheaper some time later," says Nader. "Experience is often developed the hard way. Just don't over do it, and things will work out." Rule #4 is the most important: don't forget that this is a hobby. "If you look at it as an investment, you will probably make more money by putting it in the bank, and sitting at home. Collect for the fun of it! If you make some money in the process, great, use it to fund your hobby." And Rule #5, "if it isn't fun, don't do it anymore. Collect something else, or do something else." Like most hobby rules, these are unwritten, but Nader said they "are the ones we try to go by."

Reed D. Andrew of the Society of Root Beer Cans and Bottles, said that someone wishing to begin in the root beer collecting hobby should buy what's in the store first. "There are many fine paper labels, ACLs, and cans currently on the market." Antique malls are also good places to begin: "If you have a little dough you can pick up nifty old bottles (Dad's, Dr. Swett's, Mason's, Hires) for two to ten dollars a piece." Of course, there are other places for discovering cans and bottles, if you're brave enough. "I have dug up cans in rubbish piles and have found old bottles in abandoned buildings. Finding them all by yourself is the greatest adventure of all. That is the way I prefer to find additions to my collection," said Andrew. His newsletter reporting new finds and other interesting tidbits about collecting is available from Society of Root Beer Cans & Bottles 1220 Cedar Ave. Bsmt, Provo, Utah 84604, USA The Society also maintains a Web page on the Internet's World Wide Web at http://www.byu.edu/~rdandrew.

At last count, Dave Nader's *Root Beer Float* collector's newsletter was being sent to people in twenty-seven states and Canada. The publication gets practically no publicity; only word of mouth and an Internet Web site draw in subscribers. The bi-monthly newsletter is free for the asking, but Nader does ask for help with postage. You can contact The Root Beer Float at P.O. Box 571, Lake Geneva, Wisconsin 53147.

As millions of people know, the Internet's World Wide Web is the place to go for information on just about any subject you wish to explore. And if you're seeking a root beer fix, it's definitely a one-stop shop. You can't drink it here, of course, but you can totally immerse yourself in everything root beer: from brewpubs, flavoring supply outlets and old-fashioned recipes, to photos of root beer bottles, mugs, and even vintage advertisements. Some of the pages belong to soft drink companies and some are the work of hobbyists or businesses. Point your browser to http://www.primo.com/portfiles/root.html for a look at the award-winning labels and bottles that Primo Angeli, Incorporated, designed for Henry Weinhardt's root beer (these designs won Best of Show in 1995 at the Beverage Packaging Global Design Awards). Or try http://www.islandnet.com/~kpolsson/

mugs.htm for a visual trip through Ken Polsson's collection of root beer mugs. Interested in flavorings to add to your own home-brewed root beer? Try Hoptech at http://www.hoptech.com/rootbeer.html or the Homebrewer's Outpost at http://homebrewers.com/catalog/softdrinkmixes.html. There's a whole world related to root beer out there on the Internet. There are other sites of interest listed later in this book. You can also run a comprehensive search via one of the Internet's search engines (also listed further on) using "root beer" as a key word. Don't be surprised if you find more than you can handle!

The Internet is more than just the World Wide Web, however. If you are looking for root beer lovers to converse with, try joining one of the drink-related newsgroups such as alt.beer, alt.drink, alt.food or rec.crafts.brewing. A brief message posted to one of these groups is guaranteed to receive some kind of reply and the conversation that results is sure to be interesting. If you have access to FidoNet, another collection of newsgroups in a vein similar to the Internet, try visiting the Herbs-N-Such, Gourmet, Cooking or Home-Cooking conferences.

ROOT BEER ADVENTURES

W hen you spend any great amount of time absorbed in a project - gathering information, researching, digging for background, interviewing people and generally being totally immersed in your subject, as I did with this book - you run the risk of information overload, of becoming so enmeshed in following leads, tiny disconnected threads and hopefully related possibilities that you end up with more information than you can possibly condense into one volume. That didn't happen with this book.

If I had been researching Coca-Cola, for instance, or beer, or wine, I would have found a plethora of references everywhere I looked. But root beer is an altogether different story. This "quiet" soda, this barely regarded, but much-loved soft drink, is largely unsung. You will be hard-pressed to find articles written about it (unless you're a regular reader of beverage trade magazines), and television commercials for root beer are rarely scheduled. Yet, nearly every major soft drink manufacturer produces a root beer product, and anywhere you go you will find it on the menu or in vending machines. Root beer is a paradox, obscure and yet well-known at the same time. How do you research something as slippery as a paradox? How do you find information on a subject that doesn't even have its own encyclopedia entry? You dig and you hunt and you never give up, that's how.

In researching this book, I was forced to sift the wheat from the chaff, myth from reality. I found myself led down roads I thought would be promising, only to find disappointing dead ends. For instance, while searching the Internet for root beer related information, I discovered several links to businesses that had root beer in their name, but their trade actually had nothing to do with the soft drink itself. Root Beer Comics, a comic book store, was one (http://www.inkless.com/rbcomics.html). I even found a reference to something called a root beer chair, which was - just as you guessed - a wooden chair. One Web page featured a *Hagar the Horrible* comic strip which had a root beer theme, and another mentioned the fact that Snoopy, the famous comic strip beagle, loves root beer. Duke University's John W. Hartman Center World Wide Web site even displays a 1933 advertisement for Hires Root Beer. But, amid the obscure references I did manage to find some golden tidbits. Some are true and some are legend, but all are part of the root beer adventure.

Root beer pops up in the oddest places, buried in the tales of our past. In the 1850's, Harriet Tubman, a Maryland slave who would go down in history as a "conductor" of the Underground Railroad, sold homemade pies, gingerbread and root beer to support herself while serving as a nurse, spy and scout for the Union government. Tubman wasn't the only woman who used root beer to survive. Dorothy Molter, who ran a backwoods resort in northern Minnesota from 1930-1986, made root beer with the help of ice carved from the frozen waters of Knife Lake. She sold the root beer to passing fishermen, earning herself the title of "The Root Beer Lady." Someone even wrote a book about her.

And, of course, we can't forget Juan Ponce de Leon, who accompanied Christopher Columbus on his second voyage to America in 1493. Though there is no root beer in the story of Ponce de Leon, there is the tale of his search for a mysterious fountain. Ponce de Leon conquered Puerto Rico (then called Boriquen) for Spain and served as governor of the island from 1510 to 1512. The locals there told him stories of an island called Bimini, whose location was described only as "somewhere north of Cuba." On this island, they said, flowed the fountain of youth, a natural spring whose waters had the magical power to restore youth. Ponce de Leon was taken with the legend and in 1512 he secured permission from the king of Spain to search out, conquer, and colonize Bimini. He sailed the next year and, on March 27, sighted the eastern shore of Florida, which he believed to be Bimini. Ponce de Leon never did find the Fountain of Youth, but his search is part of our long fascination with carbonated mineral waters, precursors of today's soft drinks.

Root beer and legends seem to go together. There's one story about a sailor who was exiled to a desert island as punishment for stealing the ship captain's beer. To remind him of what he had done to deserve being marooned alone on a tiny outcropping in the middle of the ocean, the captain left him with one bottle of beer. After several days, thirsty and delirious, he drank half the bottle and passed out. While he was unconscious a seed, carried on warm tropical winds, found its way into the bottle and began to sprout. Island natives found the man and his bottle, tasted the strange liquid and so was born the "root of the beer" or root beer.

Beyond the myths and legends is the simple truth that root beer drinkers everywhere know: root beer is growing in popularity. Its second cousin status, its position on the low end of the soft drink totem pole, is a place it holds in number only. Max Clough of the Thomas Kemper Soda Company told the *Puget Sound Business Journal* that "people in the Northeast complained that they couldn't get their root beer during the last blizzard because it was freezing in the trucks. We had to air freight it in. That's a great sign." The MTV television network's summer 1996 Beach House/Mug Root Beer promotion drew more than 10,000 calls in one day, proving that the oldest of the soft drinks is a perennial favorite, one whose real fame is only just beginning.

So, go out and buy a six pack, hoist a can and drink deep. Root beer is back in style - as if it ever really wasn't!

A Celebration of America's Best-Loved Soft Drink

 # ROOT BEER RECIPES

SHORT-CUT ROOT BEER
Non-Alcoholic

Here's a way to experience root beer that you make yourself without having to go through all of the brewing, fermenting and waiting that using yeast entails.

2 cups sugar
1 cup water
root beer extract
soda
water
ice

Boil 2 cups of sugar in one cup of water for five minutes or until the sugar is dissolved. Set the mixture aside to cool, then pour into a container and refrigerate. Whenever you're ready for root beer, add one to two teaspoons of the sugar syrup to one glass of carbonated water. Then add root beer extract to taste.

NO-FIZZ ROOT BEER
Non-Alcoholic
Makes: 2-6 cups

Experience root beer the way it was originally enjoyed, without the carbonation that we're so used to these days.

1/4 tablespoon root beer extract
12 ounces water
2 tablespoons sugar

Add 1/4 tablespoon of root beer extract to 12 ounces of water. Stir in 2 tablespoons of sugar or other sweetener. Refrigerate and serve.

EASY ROOT BEER

Serves: 1 Non-Alcoholic

Like the fellow in the brewery shop said, "making root beer isn't a Gilbert and Sullivan production." All you need is sugar, yeast, extract and water. This recipe takes about ten minutes to complete and anywhere from 48 hours to two weeks to ferment. Keep an eye on the finished bottles and test the carbonation level often by cracking the cap. When you get a good hiss of air, it's ready.

2 cups sugar
1 teaspoon yeast
2 tablespoons root beer extract

Place ingredients in a gallon jug with approximately one quart of very warm water. Stir until all ingredients are well mixed. Finish filling the jug with warm water and place the lid on the bottle. Let stand 48 hours to two weeks, then refrigerate.

ORIGINAL OLD-TIME ROOT BEER

Serves: Approximately 4
Non-Alcoholic

This recipe resulted from hours of study and way too much time learning about the natural way to make root beer. It takes you back over one hundred years to the way they used to do it at home, before root beer became something processed and canned on a supermarket shelf. The result of this recipe is a drink that is unlike any root beer beverage you've tasted before.

3 ounces sassafras bark, dried
2 ounces sarsaparilla, dried
1 ounces dandelion root, dried
1 ounces burdock root, dried
1/2 ounce ground ginger
1/2 ounce ground cinnamon
1/2 ounce ground nutmeg
1/4 ounce orange peel, dried

Mix together all ingredients and store in a tightly closed container. In a large pot, combine 1 quart of water and 4 tablespoons of dry mixture. Bring to a boil, cover and simmer for 15 to 20 minutes. Strain and sweeten with honey, if needed. If desired, chill and add carbonated water.

A Celebration of America's Best-Loved Soft Drink

BREWER BROTHERS ROOT BEER
Non-Alcoholic

There is no one way to make root beer. Toss in a few different ingredients and you can sharply change the taste of what you're brewing. This little concoction adds some natural sweeteners, plus yeast. Try it and see what happens. Just remember to watch the fermentation process closely to avoid exploding bottles.

1 ounce sarsaparilla
1 ounce sassafras
1 ounce ginger root
1 ounce birch bark
2 pounds molasses
2 pounds honey
1 pounds sugar
2 packets pasteur champagne yeast

Boil sugar and spices in 2 gallons of water for 30 minutes. Allow the mixture to cool and then add 2 packets of Pasteur Champagne yeast. Bottle and store in a warm place. After 3 days, check the carbonation level. Once carbonation is at an acceptable level, chill the root beer. If chilled nearly to the freezing level, the fermentation process will stop. Store in a cool place. Extract can be added for taste, if desired.

ANCIENT ROOT BEER
Non-Alcoholic
Makes 15 gallons

This recipe shows that even if you leave out a couple of ingredients, you'll still come up with something acceptable to drink. Perhaps adding too many ingredients just took too long so our forefathers decided to shorten up the list.

1& 1/2 gallon molasses
1/4 pound sassafras bark, bruised
1/4 pound wintergreen bark
1/4 pound sarsaparilla root
1/2 pint fresh yeast
water

Bring 5 gallons of water to a boil, then add 1& 1/2 gallons of molasses. Allow the mixture to stand for 2-3 hours. Add sassafras bark, wintergreen bark, sarsaparilla root and yeast. Add enough water to make 15 gallons. Store in a warm place for 12 hours. Draw and bottle mixture, then store in a cool place.

DRAFT STYLE ROOT BEER
Non-Alcoholic

If you want to make a large quantity of root beer, this is the recipe for you. Just remember to leave an inch of space at the top of each bottle you fill.

1 bottle root beer concentrate
4.4 pounds sugar
5 gallons warm water
3/4 teaspoon fresh household yeast
refillable soda bottles

Add 1 bottle root beer concentrate to 4.4 pounds of sugar and dissolve in 5 gallons warm water. Add 3/4 teaspoon of fresh household yeast to warm water and let stand until dissolved. Add yeast to this mixture and stir well. Bottle by filling refillable soda bottles to within 1 inch from the top. Place bottles in a warm place (72-78 degrees F) for one week to allow carbonation. Move bottles to a cold location (refrigerator) to prevent excess carbonation.

WILD CHERRY ROOT BEER
Makes 13 gallons Non-Alcoholic

Somebody must have had some spare Wild Cherry Bark lying around. It's the only reason I can think of for adding that ingredient to the mixture. The taste, however, is definitely different and not altogether unappealing. This recipe makes about thirteen gallons, so make sure you like it before you go all out.

2 & 1/2 ounces sassafras
1 & 1/2 ounces wild cherry bark
1 & 1/2 ounces allspice
2 & 1/2 ounces wintergreen bark
1/2 ounce hops
1/2 ounce coriander seed
2 gallons molasses
1 pint yeast

Pour boiling water on sassafras, wild cherry bark, allspice, wintergreen bark, hops, coriander seed and molasses. Allow the mixture to stand for 1 day. Strain mixture, add 1 pt. yeast and enough water to make 13 gallons. Allow to stand, bottle after 24 hours.

A Celebration of America's Best-Loved Soft Drink

MOLASSES ROOT BEER
Non-Alcoholic
Makes 5 gallons

 2 ounces root beer extract
 1 1/2 cups (12 oz) of molasses
 4 lb. brown sugar
 1 cup vanilla extract
 1/4 teaspoon of ale yeast

Combine ingredients, bottle and let sit at room temperature for 48 hours, then refrigerate and enjoy.

REALLY LONG, REALLY COMPLICATED ROOT BEER
Alcoholic

Root Beer brewing doesn't have to be hard, unfortunately some folks like to concoct long, involved recipes like this one just to make it look like something complicated. If you can find all of these ingredients and you have the patience to boil all this for 12 hours then go ahead, knock yourself out.

 1 pound sarsaparilla
 1/4 pound spicewood
 1/2 pound guaiacum chips
 1/8 pound birch bark
 1/4 ounce ginger
 2 ounces sassafras
 1/4 ounces prickly ash bark
 1/2 ounce hops

Combine ingredients, add sufficient water and boil slowly for 12 hours. To the remaining approximately 3 gallons, add 4 ounces tincture of ginger, 1/2 ounce oil of wintergreen and 1 pint alcohol. Take 1 quart and mix in 8 ounces molasses, 2 & 1/2 gallons of water, and 4 ounces of yeast and mix. Bottle.

1910 ROOT BEER
Non-Alcoholic

One of the few recipes I found that actually dates back to the early 1900's, this one shows that the natural way was and still is the way to go.

- 1 cake yeast, compressed
- 5 pounds sugar
- 2 ounces sassafras root
- 2 ounces juniper berries
- 1 ounce hops
- 1 ounce ginger root
- 1 ounce dandelion root
- 2 ounce wintergreen
- 4 gallons water

Wash roots in cold water. Add crushed juniper berries, hops and ginger root. Pour 8 quarts boiling water over root mixture and boil slowly for 20 minutes. Strain through a fine strainer, then add sugar and remaining 8 quarts of water. Allow mixture to settle, then strain and bottle. Cork tightly. Keep in a warm place 5-6 hours, then store in a cool place.

EARLY AMERICAN ROOT BEER
Non-Alcoholic
Makes: 2 1/4 gallons

Another oldie but goodie, this recipe proves that to do it right, you've got to allow the roots and herbs to simmer for 12 hours to extract the true flavor. The result is worth it.

- 2 gallons water
- 1 & 1/2 cups honey
- 3 tablespoons ground sarsaparilla
- 1 tablespoon sassafras
- 1 heaping tablespoon hops
- 1/4 teaspoon ground coriander
- 1/4 teaspoon wintergreen extract
- 1/4 teaspoon yeast

Place sarsaparilla, sassafras, hops and coriander into a stainless steel pan, cover with water and bring to a boil. Reduce heat and simmer for 12 hours. Strain out the solids and add the liquid to 2 gallons of water which has been boiled and cooled to a lukewarm temperature. Stir in honey, wintergreen extract and yeast dissolved in 2/3 cup warm water. Stir mixture thoroughly and allow to stand for 4-5 hours. Siphon off root beer and bottle, store in a cool place.

FOUNTAIN BLEND ROOT BEER
Non-Alcoholic

No roots in this one, just a modern recipe for one of America's best loved drinks. They say the preservative is necessary, but I shudder to think that science has to invade art.

6 pounds granular sugar
1 gallon spring water
2 ounces root beer flavoring
1 ounce sodium benzoate preservative
chilled club soda

Combine 64 ounces of spring water with sodium benzoate and mix until dissolved. Add 6 pounds of granular sugar. Fill a 5 gallon mixing container to the one gallon level and blend until sugar is completely dissolved. Add 2 ounces of root beer extract (to yield 1 gallon of root beer syrup). Chill syrup for 2 hours. Measure 2 ounces of root beer syrup into a mixing container. Add 10 ounces of chilled club soda. Blend well.

OLD MODERN ROOT BEER
Non-Alcoholic

When you split the difference, using a little bit of old world ingredients and a little bit of the new, this is the result.

4 lb 12 oz sugar, granulated
1 bottle root beer extract
4 gal (64 fl oz) water, lukewarm
3/4 tsp Fleischman's active dry yeast
1 cup water, lukewarm

Shake extract bottle well. Pour extract over sugar and mix. Dissolve in 4 gal 64 fl oz lukewarm water. Mix 3/4 teaspoon of yeast in 1 cup lukewarm water and let stand 5 minutes. Bottle immediately, filling bottle to within 1/2 inch of top. Place bottles in a warm place until carbonation is complete (5-7 days) Store in a cool place. Refrigerate before opening.

SHANGHAI ROOT BEER
Alcoholic Serves: 1

I call this one Shanghai Root Beer because you'll feel like you've been shanghaied if you drink it as though it were regular root beer.

1 ounce Galliano
1 ounce Kahlua club soda or beer to fill.

Frost one empty beer mug. Mix Galliano and Kahlua in mug, and fill with club soda or beer.

SCHNAPPY ROOT BEER
Alcoholic

Okay, I had never heard of root beer schnapps before this recipe crossed my desk (maybe I'm not the connoisseur I think I am). The completed drink has a definite snap to it, but I'm not sure if it's the schnapps, the bourbon or the Sambuca that does it.

1 shot bourbon
2 shots Coca-Cola or Pepsi
1/2 shot root beer schnapps
1/2 shot Sambuca

Combine Bourbon, Coca-cola or Pepsi, root beer schnapps and Sambuca in a frosted mug and serve.

ROOT BEER WITH A KICK
Alcoholic Serves: 1

2 ounces root beer schnapps
10 ounces root beer

What do you know? There's real root beer in this one! The kick from the schnapps is unmistakable, however. Mix ingredients in a frosted mug and serve over ice.

REAL BEER ROOT BEER
Alcoholic Serves: 1

The original root beer created by Charles Hires was mildly alcoholic, but had no real beer in it. This recipe changes all that. Just add your favorite brew.

1 cup beer
1 shot glass
root beer schnapps

Mix 1 cup of beer with 1 shot glass of root beer schnapps and let stand 2 minutes. Serve.

ROOT BEER COCKTAIL
Alcoholic Serves: 1

This is what happens when you really jazz up root beer. Whoever decided to include the egg must have been experiencing a slow day.

2 ounces gin
2 ounces root beer
1/2 lemon, squeezed juice
1 whole egg
1 teaspoon powdered sugar

Mix all ingredients with ice. Strain into a highball glass. Add ice as needed and serve.

SAN DIEGO-STYLE ROOT BEER
Alcoholic Serves 1

Here in San Diego, America's Finest City, we like things that fizz like the surf. Reminds us that we live just minutes from the grand Pacific Ocean. Put this recipe together just before sunset, drag your chair out on the deck overlooking the water, put on some David Sanborn and you've found heaven.

1 ounce coffee liqueur

1 ounce Galliano

2 ounces club soda

1 ounce Coca-Cola

splash of beer (optional)

Combine ingredients in a highball glass, add ice and serve.

ROBITUSSIN
Alcoholic Serves: 1

Despite the name, this drink doesn't actually resemble anything medicinal, though it might end up curing your sore throat if you have one.

1 & 1/2 ounce cherry vodka

1 & 1/2 ounce root beer schnapps

Mix ingredients and serve without ice for best taste.

FOURTH OF JULY FLOAT
Serves: 1 Non-Alcoholic

When most people think of root beer, they think of the root beer float, a traditional summertime drink that goes great with picnics, fireworks and family get-togethers. The neat thing about this drink is that even though it's called a Fourth of July Float, it fits in well in any season. For a fun change use Neapolitan ice cream.

1/4 cup root beer

1 teaspoon milk

scoop vanilla ice cream

Place 1/4 cup root beer and 1 teaspoon of milk in a 10 oz. glass. Add a large scoop of vanilla ice cream and stir slightly. Add 3/4 cup more of root beer to fill.

MARION'S ROOT BEER JELLO
Makes 2 cups

Tired of the same old Jello flavors? Try this for a change and you may never go back. My mother, who created this recipe especially for this book, said to tell you that adding mixed fruit right before you chill the finished product is a neat way to give this dish a little extra zing.

2 cups water
1 package unflavored gelatin (7 grams)
1/3 cup sugar
1 & 1/2 teaspoon root beer extract

In 1/2 cup of cold water, stir in one package (about 7 grams) of unflavored gelatin and allow to sit for five minutes. In a saucepan, bring 1& 1/2 cups of water to a boil and then pour into gelatin mixture. Add 1/3 cup of sugar and 1 & 1/2 teaspoons of root beer extract. Mix well and refrigerate until firm (2-3 hours.)

ROOT BEER BAKED BEANS
Serves: 6

Yes, you can do something with root beer besides drinking it. For something different and delicious, try this one out. You won't be disappointed.

2 strips bacon, diced
1 small onion, diced
36 ounces baked beans
1/2 cup root beer
1/4 cup Worcestershire sauce
1/2 teaspoon dry mustard
3 drops hot pepper sauce
pinch of ground pepper
pinch of garlic
pinch of brown sugar

Cook bacon with onion in a medium-sized saucepan until bacon is brown and crisp. Add remaining ingredients. Heat to a boil; reduce heat and simmer, stirring often, until slightly thickened, 20 minutes.

NO COOK ROOT BEER ICE CREAM

We've all heard of making Root Beer floats, but what about Root Beer ice cream?

3 cups sugar
1 teaspoon salt
4 teaspoons Root Beer extract
3 quarts half and half

Dissolve sugar and salt in 1 quart of half and half in the freezing unit. Pour in the remaining ingredients. Churn in electric or hand crank ice cream freezer.

ROOT BEER CAKE

This is a true treat that the whole family will flip over. Try adding walnuts or pecans to the topping for extra zing.

2 cups plain flour
2 cups sugar
1 cup root beer
3 cubes margarine
1/2 cup milk
1 teaspoon baking soda
1 teaspoon vanilla
1/2 teaspoon salt
2 eggs
1 & 1/2 cups miniature marshmallows

Mix 2 cups flour with two cups of sugar. In a saucepan, combine 1 cup root beer and two cubes of margarine, bring to a boil and add to the flour mixture. Stir well. Add in 1/2 cup milk, 1 teaspoon baking soda, 1 teaspoon vanilla, 1/2 teaspoon salt and two eggs. Blend. If desired, stir in 1& 1/2 cups of miniature marshmallows to the mixture. Bake in a 9x12 pan at 325F for thirty minutes. For a great topping, use one cube of margarine and 1/3 cup of root beer, bring to a boil and add one box of confectioner's sugar. Mix and pour over cake while hot.

ROOT BEER FROSTING

Makes: enough for one 8 inch by 8 inch by 2 inch cake

If you're not brave enough to try a root beer cake, consider this frosting instead. It goes great on a vanilla cake, but feel free to experiment.

1/4 cup butter, margarine or vegetable shortening
1/8 teaspoon salt
2 cups of confectioners' sugar
about 4 tablespoons cream or milk
1 teaspoon root beer extract

Work the butter and salt with a spoon or electric beater until fluffy and creamy. Add in confectioners' sugar and cream alternately, while continuing to stir with spoon or beat. Add only enough cream to achieve spreading consistency. Add the vanilla, and spread on cake.

ROOT BEER SNO-CONES

On a hot day there's nothing better than a cool treat. Try this variation on an old favorite, the sno-cone. You can adjust the amounts as needed to make more or less.

2 cups
2 cups crushed/shaved ice
1 can Root Beer

Divide crushed ice between cups. Fill cups with root beer.

FROZEN FLOATS (Root Beer Popsicles)

I'm a sucker for ice cream and I'm always trying to devise new ways of enjoying it. Tired of making root beer floats, I decided to try root beer popsicles instead. Kids will love them and so will everyone else in the family.

1 can root beer
vanilla ice cream
1/2 cup milk
1 ice cube tray or other types of container

Combine one can of root beer, half cup milk and several scoops of vanilla ice cream in a blender. Blend until creamy. Pour into an ice cube tray. Freeze. As mixture hardens, insert popsicle sticks into each cube. Once frozen, separate cubes with a butter knife and remove from container.

ROOT BEER HAM

Once you start making and drinking root beer, you will begin to dream up ways in which the drink can be used in everyday cooking. For an interesting, sweet and totally unexpected taste treat, try this recipe for Root Beer Ham.

1 five pound boneless ham
3 tablespoons brown sugar
1/4 cup root beer

Place the ham, pre-cooked, in a shallow baking pan. Combine three tablespoons of brown sugar with 1/4 cup of root beer and sprinkle over the ham. Cover ham with aluminum foil (optional) and bake at 350F for 1 & 1/2 to 2 hours. If covered, uncover for the last fifteen minutes of cooking time.

ROOT BEER CAKE
Serves 10-12

A true Root Beer lover can't pass up a chance to make this cake. Trust me, I've tried. Simple, yet effective, this recipe turns a boring white cake into a Root Beer extravaganza.

1 package white/yellow cake mix
1 small package instant vanilla pudding
4 eggs
3/4 cup vegetable oil
1 teaspoon nutmeg
1 teaspoon root beer extract

Mix all ingredients together in the order listed above. Beat on low for five minutes. Pour into well greased angel food cake pan and bake for 45 minutes at 350 degrees. After cake has cooled, sprinkle top with powdered sugar.

ROOT BEER POUND CAKE
Serves 8-10

    3 cups sugar
    1 1/2 cups (3 sticks) margarine or butter
    5 eggs
    3 cups cake flour
    3/4 cup Root Beer

In a large bowl beat sugar and margarine (or butter) with an electric mixer until light and fluffy. Add eggs and beat. Add in and beat the cake flour, a cup at a time. Add in and beat the Root Beer. Pour into greased bundt pan and bake at 325 degrees for 70 minutes. Can be topped with sifted powdered sugar.

ROOT BEER BALLS
Makes about 4 dozen

    32 vanilla wafers
    1 cup pecans, chopped
    2 tablespoons cocoa
    4 tablespoons white corn syrup
    4 tablespoons Root Beer extract
    confectioner's sugar

Crush wafers to make crumbs. Place into 1-quart mixer bowl. Blend in chopped pecans. Add cocoa, syrup and Root Beer and mix thoroughly. Coat hands with confectioner's sugar and roll mixture into 1/2" balls. Refrigerate for about one hour and then roll in confectioner's sugar.

ROOT BEER CARAMELS
Makes 48+ pieces

    4 cups sugar
    4 cups light corn syrup
    1/2 pound butter
    4 cups evaporated milk
    6 cups walnuts (optional)
    1 teaspoon Root Beer extract
    1/4 teaspoon salt

In a heavy pot cook sugar, corn syrup and butter together until 245 degrees on a medium heat. Do not remove from heat and gradually add the 4 cups evaporated milk. Do not allow mixture to stop boiling at anytime. Cook at high heat, stirring constantly until mixture returns to 245 degrees. Remove from heat and add 6 cups of nuts (do not chop) (optional). Add Root Beer extract and salt. Mix and turn into buttered pan. Allow to cool and cut into squares. Wrap individually in plastic.

ROOT BEER SUGAR COOKIES
Makes 4 dozen

I've always been a fan of the good ol' sugar cookie. Give me a plate of these and I'm in heaven. But, add in Root Beer and the common sugar cookie becomes something a little bit different.

1 cup powdered sugar
1 cup granulated sugar
2 cups margarine
1 cup oil
2 eggs
4 1/2 cups flour
1 teaspoon baking soda
1 teaspoon cream of tartar
1 teaspoon Root Beer extract

Mix all ingredients together and let stand for a few minutes. Shape into balls. Flatten with a water glass dipped in sugar. Bake at 350 degrees about 12 minutes till barely light brown around the edges.

ROOT BEER BARREL PUFFS
Makes about 3 to 4 dozen

One of my favorites is the Root Beer barrel candy that you can find at any store. Crush these up and add them to this recipe. Then just try to keep the kids away!

2/3 cup butter-flavored Crisco
1/4 cup sugar
1/4 cups brown sugar, firmly packed
1 egg
1 1/2 cups flour, unsifted
1/2 teaspoon baking powder
1/2 teaspoon salt
1/2 cup Root Beer barrel candy, crushed

Preheat oven to 350 degrees. Lightly grease baking sheets with butter-flavored Crisco. Cream butter-flavored Crisco and sugars in a large bowl at medium speed of electric mixer. Beat in egg. Combine flour, baking powder, and salt. Blend into creamed mixture and stir in crushed candy. Shape dough into small balls (about 1"). Bake for 11 to 15 minutes and remove to cooling racks.

ROOT BEER TOPPINGS

For a wonderful topping that can garnish cakes, cookies, or ice cream, crush a bag of Root Beer barrel candies and spread over your desert. What a treat for the Root Beer lover!

A Celebration of America's Best-Loved Soft Drink

ITALIAN ROOT BEER SLICES
Makes 3-4 dozen

My parents would call this sacrilege, putting Root Beer into an Italian recipe. I did it anyway. They make a great dessert, or as my Dad would say "abbondanza!".

3 cups flour, sifted
1 teaspoon salt
1 tablespoon baking powder
1/2 cup butter
1 cup sugar
1 teaspoon Root Beer extract flavoring
3 eggs

Preheat oven to 350 degrees. Sift together dry ingredients. Cream together butter, sugar and Root Beer flavoring. Beat in eggs, one at a time. Add creamed mixture to flour mixture and blend. On a cookie sheet form 2 rectangles, approximately 10" long, 4" wide, and 1 1/2" thick. Bake at 350 degrees until firm to touch, or about 35 minutes. Turn off oven. Remove from oven and cool slightly. While warm, cut into slices about 1/2" thick and separate. Return to oven to dry, about 10-20 minutes. Cool and store.

ROOT BEER CREAM PUFF RING
Serves 8-10

This is one of the more involved recipes, but it's a true delight once it's done. Adapted from the French gourmet recipe.

1 cup plus 1 tablespoon water
1/2 cup butter
1/2 teaspoon salt
1 cup flour
4 eggs
1 egg yolk
2 cups heavy cream, chilled
1 cup powdered sugar
2 teaspoons Root Beer extract
extra powdered sugar

Preheat oven to 400 degrees. In a saucepan, combine the 1 cup water, butter and salt. Bring to a boil and then remove from heat. Beat in flour with spoon. Mixture will form a ball and leave sides of pan. Remove from heat. Add whole eggs, one at a time, and mix between each addition. On baking sheet lined with brown paper, draw an 8" circle. Form a ring with dough on the inside of the circle. Bake 50 minutes. Then, using a fork, in a small bowl, beat egg yolk with the remaining 1 tablespoon water. Remove ring from oven. Brush egg mixture lightly over top of ring. Bake 5 minutes more and cool on wire rack. Meanwhile, in a medium bowl, combine cream, 1 cup powdered sugar and extract. Refrigerate, covered, for 1 hour. Place in a larger bowl of ice water and eat at high speed until stiff. With a sharp knife, split ring in half crosswise. Place bottom on serving platter. Pipe filling through a pastry bag onto cut bottom layer. Set top in place. Sprinkle with more powdered sugar.

IMPORTANT EVENTS IN THE DEVELOPMENT OF SOFT DRINKS

Reprinted with permission of the National Soft Drink Association

1798 The term "soda water" is first introduced.

1809 The first U.S. patent is issued for the manufacture of imitation mineral waters.

1815 The first soda fountain is patented.

1835 Bottled soda water is first produced in the United States.

1850 Manual hand-foot filling, corking device is first used for bottling soda water.

1851 Ginger ale is introduced in Ireland.

1861 Soft drinks are first referred to as "pop".

1874 The first ice cream soda is served.

1876 Root beer is produced in quantity for public sale.

1881 First cola-flavored beverage is introduced.

1892 The crown bottle cap is invented.

1899 The first patent for a glass blowing machine, used to produce glass bottles.

1913 Motor trucks begin to replace horse drawn carriages as delivery vehicles.

1919 Industry joins to form a national association, the American Bottlers of Carbonated Beverages.

1920 U.S. Census reports more than 5,000 bottlers in business.

Early 1920's First automatic vending machine begin to dispense soda in cups.

- 1923 Introduction of six-pack cartons called "Hom-Paks".
- 1934 Color labels are used to merchandise products.
- 1946 First diet soft drink introduced.
- 1957 First aluminum cans are introduced.
- 1962 Easy open, pull-ring tabs are first available.
- 1962 First diet cola is introduced.
- 1965 Soft drinks in cans appear in vending machines.
- 1965 Resealable tops are invented.
- 1966 American Bottlers of Carbonated Beverages renamed American Soft Drink Association.
- 1970 Plastic bottles are first used for soft drinks.
- 1973 Creation of the PET plastic bottle.
- 1981 Talking vending machines are invented.
- Mid-80's Caffeine-free and low-sodium soft drinks gain popularity.
- Early 1990's Clear colas manufactured.
- 1991 Soft drink companies being using PET bottles.
- 1993 Number of soft drink containers recycled since the first Earth Day in 1970, reaches 384 billion.

FACTS ABOUT SOFT DRINKS

- Soft drinks account for more than 27 percent of Americans' beverage consumption.
- 95% of Americans regularly consume soft drinks.
- 25% of all beverages consumed by Americans (from water to wine) are soft drinks.
- Soft drinks are consumed in more than 195 countries.
- The U.S. market includes nearly 450 different soft drinks.
- The soft drink industry employs more than 136,000 people.
- More than 600 bottlers operate across the United States.
- Nearly 78 percent of soft drinks are packaged, the remaining 22 percent are dispensed from fountains.
- In 1995, 62.6 billion soft drinks were packaged in aluminum cans, 16.8 billion were packaged PET plastic bottles, and 2.2 billion were packaged in glass bottles.
- Regular non-diet soft drinks contain about 7 to 14 percent sweeteners, the same as juices such as pineapple and orange.
- Most non-diet soft drinks are sweetened with high fructose corn syrup, sugar or a combination of both.
- Most diet soft drinks are sweetened with aspartame, a sweetener that provides less than one calorie in a 12-ounce can.

A Celebration of America's Best-Loved Soft Drink

SOFT DRINK BRAND INTRODUCTIONS IN THE U.S.

1866-1995

Vernors 1866
Hires Root Beer 1876
Dr. Pepper 1885
Coca-Cola 1886
Canada Dry Ginger Ale 1907
Cott 1914
Crush Orange 1916
A&W Root Beer 1919
IBC Root Beer 1919
Sun-drop 1928
Seven-Up 1929
Hi-Spot 1936
Diet Canada Dry Ginger Ale 1937
Squirt 1938
Wink 1947
Diet Canada Dry Tonic 1948
No Cal 1952
Schweppes Mixers 1955
Diet Squirt 1951
Tahitian Treat 1962
Crush Flavors 1963
Diet Dr Pepper 1963
Barrelhead Root Beer 1969
Diet Seven-Up 1970
Diet Vernors 1971
Diet A&W Root Beer 1974
Diet Schweppes Tonic 1975

Sunkist Orange 1977
Canada Dry Seltzers 1978
Like 1982
Sugar Free Like 1982
Schweppes Seltzers 1982
Caffeine Free Dr Pepper 1983
Diet Squirt Plus 1985
Diet Crush Orange 1985
Sunkist Natural 1985
A&W Cream Soda 1986
Citrus 7 1986
Sunkist Flavors 1986
Cherry Seven-Up 1987
Schweppes Royal Seltzers 1988
Canada Dry Sparklers 1988
Seven-Up Gold 1988
Schweppes Raspberry Ginger Ale 1988
Canada Dry Cherry Ginger Ale 1989
Canada Dry Lemon Ginger Ale 1990
Nautilus 1990
Canada Dry Cranberry Ginger Ale ... 1991
Hires Mocha 1992
Everlast 1992
Energade 1992
Schweppes Dry Grape Ginger Ale 1993
Crystal Light Low Calorie Drink 1994
Country Time RTD Hot Fill 1994
Hersheys Chocolate Drink 1995

# SOME ROOT BEER BRANDS

This list is by no means all-inclusive and is, of course, subject to change.

A&W
Cadbury Beverages USA.
6 High Ridge Park
P.O. Box 3800
Stamford, CT 06905-0800

BARQ'S FAMOUS OLDE TYME ROOT BEER
P.O. Box 1278
Biloxi, MS 39533

BERGHOFF'S ROOT BEER
17 West Adams
Chicago, IL, 60603
(312) 427-3170

CANFIELD'S ROOT BEER
A.J. Canfield Company
50 E. 89th Place
Chicago, IL 60619
(312) 483-7000

DAD'S OLD FASHIONED ROOT BEER
Monarch Company
16 Perimeter Park Drive
Atlanta, GA 30341
(404) 455-3908

DOG N' SUDS
Division of DeNovo Corporation
P.O. Box 162
Utica, MI 48138
(313) 739-1307

DR. BROWN'S ROOT BEER
Canada Dry
College Pt., NY, 11356

FILBERTS ROOT BEER
Chicago, IL 60608

FROSTIE ROOT BEER
Monarch Company
16 Perimeter Park Drive
Atlanta, GA 30341 (404) 455-3908

GRANDPA GRAF'S
Milwaukee, WI

HENRY WEINHARD'S ROOT BEER
Blitz-Weinhard Company
Portland, OR

HIRES ROOT BEER
Cadbury-Schweppes Beverages USA.
6 High Ridge Park
P.O. Box 3800
Stamford, CT 06905-0800

IBC ROOT BEER
IBC Soft Drinks
Dallas, TX

KEIKO DRAFT ROOT BEER
Oregon Brewing Company
Newport, OR 97365

KILLEBREW'S ROOT BEER
Killebrew Beverages
6885 Boudin Street
Prior Lake, MN 55372
(612) 440-9011

MARTHA'S EXCHANGE ROOT BEER
185 Main Street
Nashua, NH, 03060
(603) 883-8781

MUG ROOT BEER
Pepsi-Cola Company North America
1 Pepsi Way Somers, NY 10589
(914) 767-6000

PIRATE'S KEG
Jolt Cola Company
Dallas, TX

RJ CORR
R.J. Corr Naturals, Inc.
Chicago, IL 60610

SIOUX CITY SARSAPARILLA
McChesney & Miller
460 Crescent Blvd.
Glen Ellyn, IL

SPRECHER'S BREWING COMPANY
730 W. Oregon Street
Milwaukee, WI 53204
(414) 272-2337

STEWART'S ROOT BEER
Cable Car Beverage Company
1700 E. 68th Avenue
Denver, CO 80229
(303) 288-2212

THOMAS KEMPER ROOT BEER
310 Terry
Seattle, WA 98111
(206) 632-2202
E-mail: sodapop@echannel.com

VIRGIL'S ROOT BEER
30 Boston Post Road
Wayland, MA 01778
(508) 358-7177

WEBER'S SUPERIOR ROOT BEER
Weber's Superior Root Beer Restaurant
3817 S Peoria in
Tulsa, OK (918) 742-1082

ROOT BEER ON THE INTERNET

This listing is, of course, subject to change.

Alta Vista Internet Search
http://altavista.digital.com

The Beverage Network
www.thebevnet.com

Brew Your Own Beverages Online
http://www.onlinesu.com

Bill Swislow's Root Beer Page
http://www.mcs.net/~billsw/ii/rb.html

Bunn Coffee Hard Candy
http://www.bunn.com/fsc2.htm

Cat's Meow Herbs and Spices
http://celebrator.com/spenser/cats-meow

Charles Boggini Co. Root Beer Concentrate
http://www.chasbcola.com/rtbeer.htm

Chi-An Chien's Root Beer Page
http://www.crl.com/~cac/rbeer.html

Chuck's Homemade Ozark Root Beer
http://alpha.rollanet.org/cm3/recs/12_04.html

CooperSmith's Beverages
ttp://www.fortnet.org/~cooper/beverage.html

Copernicus Home Page
http://www.comet.chv.va.us/Copernicus/

David and Kathy Nader The Root Beer Float Newsletter
E-mail: D.K.Nader@worldnet.att.net

D&D Supply Soda Flavor Extracts
http://www.inovatec.com/DD/MISC/SOLIFLM.HTM

Excite Net Internet Search
http://www.excite.com

Gallaghers' Microbrewery
http://inet-rendezvous.com/idgs.html

Hagar The Horrible Root Beer Comic
http://www.iwaynet.net/~eaevans/rbeer.html

Hartman Center for Sales, Advertising and Marketing History http://
odyssey.lib.duke.edu/hartman/jpeg

Homebrewer's Outpost Catalog: Soft Drink Mixes
http://homebrewers.com/catalog/softdrinkmixes.html

Hop Tech Root Beer Flavoring
http://www.hoptech.com/rootbeer.html

InfoSeek Internet Search
http://www.infoseek.com

Ken's Collection of A&W Root Beer Mugs
http://www.islandnet.com/~kpolsson/mugs.htm

Lycos Internet Search
http://lycos.ca.cmu.edu/

Martha's Exchange Brewing Company
http://www.marthas.com

Mendocino Soda Pop Company
http://catalog.com/mendo/gcm/mendoroo.html

Modern Brewer Root Beer
http://www.xensei.com/users/modbrew/rootbeer.html

Pirate's Keg Root Beer
http://www.joltcola.com/nojava/jolttv/news.html

Primo Angeli, Inc. Design and Marketing
http://www.primo.com/portfiles/root.html

Sahara Coffee (root beer flavoring supply)
http://www. donna@saharacoffee.com

Shane's Root Beer Page
http://www.oz.net/~tsp/rootbeer.html

Society of Root Beer Cans and Bottles Home Page
http://www.byu.edu/~rdandrew/

Thomas Kemper Root Beer
http://www.echannel.com/thomas-kempter/rbinfo.html

Virgil's Root Beer
http://www.inovatec.com/dd/virgils/default.htm

Yahoo Internet Search
http://www.yahoo.com

ROOT BEER MEMORABILIA COLLECTOR'S MAGAZINES AND ORGANIZATIONS

A&W Merchandise
P.O. Box 32549
Euclid, OH 44132
(888) 563-8646
(A&W related merchandise, such as hats, sweatshirts, jackets, T-shirts, etc.)

Antique Bottle and Glass Collector
P.O. Box 180
East Greenville, PA 18041

Bottles and Extras
Federation of Historical Bottle Collectors
Carl Sturm
88 Sweetbriar Branch
Longwood, FL 32750-2783
(magazine of the FHBC, non profit organization devoted to historical bottles and related collectible items)

Crowncapper's Exchange
John Vetter
4300 San Juan
Fairfax, VA 22030
(official journal of the Crowncap Collectors Society International)

Gatherer Promotional Glass Collector's Organization
4595 Limestone Lane
Memphis, TN 38141
(bulletin of the PGCA, featuring glasses and mugs)

Nostalgia Publications, Inc.
21 So. Lake Drive
Hackensack, NJ 07601
(twice yearly mail auction books related to soda advertising items)

Soda Net
Painted Soda Bottle Collectors Association
8418 Hilmer Drive
La Mesa, CA 91942
(official newsletter of the PSBCA, focusing on painted soda bottle labels)

BEVERAGE SUPPLY OUTLETS

Most homebrew supply houses, though they cater to the beer and wine crowd, carry root beer extracts and accessories for brewing. This list may include some firms which don't carry root beer related products but, even so, it provides you with a place to start and the 800 number calls are free. Also try your local telephone yellow pages directory under the heading "brewing supplies".

CA - Beverage People 800-544-1867
CA - Brewers Resource 800-827-3983
CA - Great Fermentations 800-542-2520
CA - HopTech 800-379-4677
CA - South Bay Homebrew Supply 800-608-2739
CO - Highlander 800-388-3923
CT - Maltose Express 800-625-8673
FL - Hearts Homebrew Supply 800-392-8322
FL - Sebastian Brewers Supply 800-780-7837
GA - Brew Your Own Beverages 800-477-2962
GA - Brewtopia 800-540-6258
IL - The Brewer's Co-op 800-451-6348
IL - Alternative Garden Supply 800-444-2837
IL - Home Brewing Emporium 800-455-2739
KY - Brew By You 800-986-2739
MA - Beer & Wine Hobby 800-523-5423
MA - The Modern Brewer 800-736-3253
MD - Brew Masters 800-466-9557
MI - The Yeast Culture Kit Company 800-742-2110
MN - Brew and Grow 800-230-8191

MN - The Malt Shop 800-235-0026
MN - Northern Brewer 800-681-2739
MN - Wind River Brewing 800-266-4677
MO - The Home Brewery 800-321-2739
NC - Alternative Beverage 800-365-2739
NJ - The Brewmeister 800-322-3020
NJ - Red Bank Brewing Supply 800-779-7507
NM - Coyote Home Brewing Supply 800-779-2739
NY - Brewers Den 800-449-2739
NY - The Brewery 800-762-2560
NY - Hennessey Homebrew NY 800-462-7397
NY - New York Homebrew 800-966-2739
OH - The Grape & Granary 800-695-9870
PA - Brew Ha Ha 800-243-2620
SC - U-Brew 800-845-4441
TX - DeFalco's 800-216-2739
TX - Homebrew Supply of Dallas 800-270-5922
VA - HomeBrew International 800-447-4883
WA - Jim's Homebrew 800-326-7769
WA - Liberty Malt Supply 800-990-6258
WI - North Brewing Supply 800-483-7238

BrewCrafters 800-468-9678
BrewShack 800-646-2739

A Celebration of America's Best-Loved Soft Drink

BOOKS OF INTEREST

Medicinal Plants and their History by Edith Grey Wheelwright; Dover Publications; 1974.

Herbs that Heal by William A.R. Thompson, M.D.; Scribner's; 1976.

Healing Drugs: The History of Pharmacology by Margery & Howard Facklam; Facts on File; 1992.

Man's Useful Plants by Michael A. Weiner; MacMillan, 1976.

Beverages by Jacqueline Dineen; Hillside: Enslow; 1988.

Is Our Water Safe? by J. Gordon Millichap; PNB Publishers, 1995.

The Root Beer Lady: The Story of Dorothy Molter by Bob Cary; Pfeifer-Hamilton, 1993.

Soda Poppery by Stephen N. Tchudi; Scribner's, 1985.

Root Beer Advertising and Collectibles by Tom Morrison; Schiffer Publishing; 1992.

A Pictorial Guide to ACL Root Beer Bottles by Tom Morrison.

American Stoneware Bottles by David Graci; Calem Publishing; 1995.

Collecting Applied Color Label Soda Bottles; Painted Soda Bottles Collectors Association.

American Stone Ginger Beer and Root Beer Bottles by Don Yates; 1996

Guys From Space by Daniel M. Pinkwater; MacMillan, 1989 (Children's book)

Who is Root Beer? by Norma Q. Hare; Garrard, 1977 (Children's book)

Going the Moose Way Home by Jim Latimer; Scribner, 1988 (Children's book)

How Does Soda Get Into the Bottle? by Charles Oz; Simon and Schuster, 1988 (Children's book)

A Celebration of America's Best-Loved Soft Drink

HOW ABOUT ANOTHER MUG?

If you have root beer lore, stories or recipes you'd like to offer for inclusion in the next edition of *The Root Beer Book* - or if you would like information about advertising your brand of root beer or home brewing supplies in the next edition, please contact the publisher or e-mail the author at: 73733.1653@compuserve.com. Additions, corrections, etc. are also welcome.

A Celebration of America's Best-Loved Soft Drink

OTHER LIMELIGHT BOOKS BY LAURA QUARANTIELLO

ON GUARD! -
How You Can Win The War Against The Bad Guys

A vitally important book filled with essential information to help you minimize your chance of being a victim in the crime-ridden '90s. A series of primers on various types of crime gives you important information on what you can do to lessen your risk of being a victim: residential security, personal safety, firearms, arson, drugs, gangs, child abuse, child abduction and more.

On Guard! also shows you how to organize your community or neighborhood to reduce crime and make your life safer and more secure: getting organized, identifying needs, working with the police, how to report a crime, patrols, confrontations, etc. Includes crime reporting forms which can be reproduced for your own use. On Guard is filled with the things you need to know to keep yourself and your family as safe as possible in the high risk '90s!

ISBN: 0936653-50-7 $17.95

CYBER CRIME -
How to Protect Yourself From Computer Criminals

Online harassment and stalking, security for your e-mail, data security, virus implantation, fraud, credit card access, your privacy, pornography - there are dozens of evils hiding out there beyoned the monitor screen. Here's the *Cyber Crime* story, and the answers to protecting your computer, yourself, your family, and your business from the cyber nasties cruising the worldwide information autobahn. It's clearly written, it's easy-to-read, it has easy-to-implement answers. It's complete with indispensable appendices, a list of online resources and a glossary. You and your computer will feel safer after you've read *Cyber Crime* and followed its suggestions!

ISBN: 0936653-74-4 $16.95

A Celebration of America's Best-Loved Soft Drink